Curious ATTRACTIONS

Essays ON *Writing*

DEBRA SPARK

THE UNIVERSITY OF MICHIGAN PRESS • ANN ARBOR

Copyright © by Debra Spark 2005
All rights reserved
Published in the United States of America by
The University of Michigan Press
Manufactured in the United States of America
ⓒ Printed on acid-free paper
2008   2007   2006   2005   4   3   2   1

A CIP catalog record for this book is available from the British Library.

Library of Congress Cataloging-in-Publication Data

Spark, Debra, 1962-
    Curious attractions : essays on fiction writing / Debra Spark.
        p.   cm.
    ISBN 0-472-09897-7 (cloth : alk. paper) — ISBN 0-472-06897-0
(pbk. : alk. paper)
        1. Fiction—Authorship.   I. Title.
    PN3355.S63   2005
    808.3—dc22   2004027417

CURIOUS ATTRACTIONS

Acknowledgments

THE ESSAYS in this volume started life as lectures for the students at Warren Wilson's MFA Program in Writing. I'm grateful to the staff and members of that program for offering me, through the years, a reason to compose my thoughts on writing matters. I'm particularly grateful to Peter Turchi, who not only hired me to teach in the program but also suggested I collect my essays in book form and then graciously led me to a publisher.

Thanks, too, to the editors of the *The Writer's Chronicle* for first publishing many of the essays in this volume; to Julie Checkoway for commissioning "Triggers in Fiction" for her anthology *Creating Fiction* (Cincinnati: Story Press, 1999); and to Charles Baxter and Peter Turchi for reprinting "Getting In and Getting Out" in *Bringing the Devil to His Knees: The Craft of Fiction and the Writing Life* (Ann Arbor: University of Michigan Press, 2001).

Finally, this book is dedicated to Garry Mitchell, my husband and always patient first reader.

THE ESSAYS and articles in this book originally appeared in the following publications: "The Trigger: What Gives Rise to a Story?" appeared in *Creating Fiction: A Complete Guide from Great Writers and Teachers of AWP*, ed. Julie Checkoway (Cincinnati: Story Press, 1999). "Getting In and Getting Out: First Words on First (and Last) Words" appeared in *The Writer's Chronicle* (May 1997) and was reprinted in *Bringing the Devil to His Knees: The Craft of Fiction and the Writing Life,* ed. Charles Baxter and Peter Turchi (Ann Arbor: University of Michigan Press, 2001). "Cry, Cry, Cry: Handling

Emotion in Fiction" appeared in *The Writer's Chronicle* (December 2000). "Curious Attractions: Magical Realism's Fate in the States" appeared in *The Writer's Chronicle* (December 1996). "Aspects of the Short Novel" appeared in *The Writer's Chronicle* (May 1999). "Stand Back" appeared in *The Writer's Chronicle* (May/Summer 2005). "Cheer Up—Why Don't You?" appeared in *The Writer's Chronicle* (October 2002).

Contents

The Trigger
WHAT GIVES RISE TO A STORY?

HERE IS my mother, in the early 1970s, with a group of Camp Fire Girls in Boston's Museum of Science. She is in a darkened (probably womblike) room with photographic displays of a developing fetus. As my mother tells it, and she does, often, in the years to come, the Camp Fire Girls are like so many kid ducks, waddling from photo to photo as she narrates the story of how babies are made. Other children, attracted by the explanation, wander over. An army of baby ducks! What my mother doesn't say but what I remember is that I am the laggard duck, ready to leave the exhibit. *The Miracle of Life,* I'm thinking. *Yeah, yeah.* Unlike the other girls, I've heard it all before. My mother is not uptight about the facts of life. For me, the cafeteria French fries, perfectly crisp and greasy, are the museum's greatest mystery. I'm wishing it were lunch. But we're still only three months into the wonder that is birth.

"OK," Terry says, finally. She is my across-the-street neighbor whom I envy for years for her early use of lipstick, her familiarity with boys and cigarettes. But today she is just a little girl. "OK," she says again to my mother, "but what I still don't *get* is how does the sperm get to the egg?"

Expectant faces. The Camp Fire Girls are now a different sort of baby bird. They are nestlings, necks craned upward, ready for a final worm of knowledge to be dropped into their open beaks. "Yeah," they might be chirping, "what about *that?*"

"OK," my mother says, brightly, "OK, everybody! Lunch!"

There is, after all, the moment of conception, and then there's the moment of conception, which no one wants to *explain,* good God, especially to children.

And so . . . with writing and the simple, yet hopelessly awkward question of where things start. Simple because there's an easy enough answer to "Where did *that* come from?" And the answer is, "Oh, an anecdote I heard, an image that came to me, a crazy article I started (but didn't really finish) in the newspaper." And hard because that's not the full story. It leaves out what my mother left out, and I don't mean the mechanics of sex but the whole messy issue of attraction.

MY HABIT, when writing about writing, is to proceed by a sort of benign plagiarism. I take the question at hand and get on the horn with my writer friends, make *them* answer. Once I've found a way to embroider their quotes together, I have my essay. But when I pose the "What gives rise to a story?" question, half my friends answer with irritable "I dunno"s. And who can blame them? Talking about the origin of a story is a bit like talking about the origin of a successful relationship. It only makes narrative sense in hindsight. ("At first, I thought he was such a jerk, but then . . .") Ideas for stories, until they prove themselves, are just another bad date, another fruitless notion flitting through the brain. ("At first, I thought nothing of the idea. The truth was . . .")

And there are other reasons we hesitate to talk about story origins. One is that it's not like talking about, say, point of view. It isn't an issue only of craft but of psychology. Ours. And we may want to keep that hidden. What's more, such talk seems presumptuous. Sure, John Updike can do it, but the rest of us—baby writers, all of us, we're all always baby writers—may feel like we're assuming too much when we talk about our process. We're assuming we're real writers, and as soon as we do that, we're bound to be punished for hubris. The punishment, naturally enough, will be that "it" will be taken away. Inspiration will flee. Permanently.

I went back to my old high school, recently, to sit on a panel with other writers. We were asked to talk about narrative, our individual narrative processes. I had a fuzzy hold on what this meant. I kept thinking, "My narrative process? You mean, how *I* became a story?" Then the youngest among us confessed that the question discomfited her, for she feared that introspection would ruin everything, destroy the magic. And I thought, "Yes, *that's* why I can't make myself understand the question: because I don't want to answer."

Just because I don't want to tell, though, doesn't mean I don't want to hear. I'd have abandoned all thoughts of French fries if I thought my mother was going to answer Terry's question. The truth is: I *like* hearing how people got their story ideas, just as I like hearing about how couples met. The same properties of attraction and repulsion, interest and doubt, seem to be at play. Then, there are the wrong turns and misperceptions along the path from there to *here*— here being the point at which the tale is finished and the story of the story has its own narrative.

Not that this knowledge helps me, exactly, when I sit down to write. After all, anything can occasion a story: an overheard conversation, image, sentence, family story, or book. Triggers are ubiquitous. They're also idiosyncratic: one person's method is never going to instruct another in how to go about "finding" a trigger.

My mother and me, on the phone, twenty years ago:

> *My mother:* I met your father at a Hillel mixer, so why don't you just head over to—
> *Me:* No, Ma, no. You just don't *get* it.

Still, triggers have some common characteristics—not in content as much as form. And we can learn something by looking at these shared traits. Perhaps we can even discover markers that will suggest whether our seeds have the potential to grow and blossom.

JOHN FOWLES'S *The French Lieutenant's Woman* started with a visual image: a woman standing at the end of a quay and staring out to sea. "That was all," Fowles writes in "Notes on an Unfinished Novel." "This image rose in my mind one morning when I was still in bed half asleep. It corresponded to no actual incident in my life (or in art) that I can recall."[1]

According to Henry James, Ivan Turgenev's fiction started with "the vision of some person or persons, who hovered before him, soliciting him."[2] These were characters whom Turgenev imagined fully, in all their existential complexity. Similarly, Joan Didion's *Play It as It Lays* began with a "picture in the mind," an image of a woman in a white halter dress walking across a Las Vegas casino to pick up a house phone. "Who is paging her?" Didion wonders aloud in her famous essay "Why I Write." "Why is she here to be paged? How exactly did she come to this?" Unlike Fowles's image, Didion's came from "real" life. One day, while sitting in a casino, Didion saw a vaguely familiar woman paged to a phone. Didion explains that "it was precisely this moment in Las Vegas that made *Play It as It Lays* begin to tell itself to me."[3]

But plenty of curious images, real or imagined, don't trigger stories. Some good material becomes . . . nothing. For example, yesterday, my husband, two friends, and I walked by a deer's head in the bed of a pickup. The head was unmounted, severed from its body, staring pointlessly up at the sky. Last week, I had lunch with a friend, and the squirming legs of the ladybug she found in her salad looked like an animated false eyelash. I don't feel inclined to embroider these images with anything more than a simile.

But these two friends from yesterday: one is an old friend of my husband's, the other is his lover of two years. They both have AIDS. The lover has a rather florid face. I don't know why he's so red. Perhaps it's just his complexion, or maybe the drugs he's taking. His wife died four years ago; he'd infected her with the virus. I sometimes think the red of his face is a form of combustion. He's aflame with grief and guilt. Both emotions—he doesn't need to say it, it's too clear—are consuming him. I wonder, I can't stop wondering, how it all worked out. The marriage, I mean. Was he always openly gay? Did they have an agreement? Or did he lead two entirely separate lives? The man and his wife were together for thirty years and had two children, whom he still sees on a weekly basis. Do they blame him for their mother's death? Or are they touched, as I am, by how he speaks of how much he misses her? He mentions that in the end a Kaposi's sarcoma grew over her eye, so she couldn't quite open the lid. But I wait for him to volunteer all this. I don't ask much.

What I do ask is, "How did you become an architect?"

His lover says, "Watch out. She's a writer, anything you tell her might go into a story."

I think: The dirt on how he chose a profession? No. Though I *can* see plundering his life for fiction. I'd have only to answer the questions I'll never ask. So a generalization that *might* help: triggers give rise to questions. They're "triggers" *because* they're incomplete, *because* they require elaboration. The red of that man's face lcads me to the heart of what I most wonder about his marriage, and since I won't ask, it leads me to a mystery that only my imagination can resolve.

Melanie Rae Thon says that her story "Punishment" sprang from "a double mystery."[4] While reading an article about slavery, Thon came across a sentence about a woman hung for the murder of her master's son. Thon first wanted to know what the article didn't say: whether the woman did it. When Thon had pursued the fictional version of the slave's life long enough to realize she *had,* Thon wanted to know *why.* The answer seems easy to me. I'd say "hateful repression" and leave it at that. What's incomplete for one person isn't necessarily incomplete for another, which is why the anecdote is a trigger for Thon and not for me. On hearing the basic facts, I don't ask a question. Of course, this doesn't mean I wouldn't want to read Thon's story, just that I don't have the curiosity necessary to write it.

MOST PEOPLE who have tried to write—and shared the fact, if not the product, of their efforts with others—have at one time had an acquaintance lean over a dinner table and confide, "Oh, I have a great story idea for you." This happened to me just last night. I was with a group of friends, most of them young Ph.D.s, talking about the academic job market. One friend—a hip, supersmart English professor, given to saying things like "Man, Thomas Hardy rocks my world"— encouraged another, a French instructor, about her job prospects: "You've got great publications, you've been teaching in a good school, and now you're going to run an overseas program." The French instructor smiled dismissively, in the way of those uneasy receiving compliments. "I should be your agent," the English professor added.

"It's going to happen soon," the French instructor enthused, "agents for Ph.D.s!"

The English professor turned to me, "Debra, this is a *great* idea for a novel. This would make a *great* farce."

She wasn't truly serious, and it's just as well, for ideas like this are invariably *not* great. Packaged up, unmysterious, they begin and end life as a dinner anecdote, unable to grow into fiction because the work of comprehending the funny, queer, horrible, or touching moment has already been done by the teller.

Joyce Carol Oates's disturbing story "Where Are You Going, Where Have You Been?" was inspired by an article about a serial murderer known as the Pied Piper of Tucson. When Oates's story became the movie *Smooth Talk,* Oates published a short essay in which she recalled purposely not reading the full account of the Pied Piper since she didn't want to be "distracted by too much detail."[5]

Now, obviously we need to have a decent grasp on the world to write well. At the same time, reality—at least at the moment of germination—*can* hamper the imagination. This realization is presumably behind Virginia Woolf's claim that for the writer, "There must be great freedom from reality."[6]

People sometimes say that the problem with writing from life, with using autobiographical material, is the instinct for veracity: we can't stop ourselves from being true to the experience, even when that sort of truth is no good for the story. The problem may actually be that a true story provides too much material; it doesn't leave enough out. Henry James held this to be so. "Such," he wrote, "is the interesting truth about the stray suggestion, the wandering word, the vague echo, at touch of which the novelist's imagination winces as at the prick of some sharp point: its virtue is all in its needle-like quality, the power to penetrate as finely as possible." Anything more than this, and the effect is ruined, and if the suggestion is offered "designedly," as James puts it, "one is sure to be given too much."[7]

IN "MAKING Up Stories," Joan Didion reveals that Joseph Heller's most famous novel began as a line so mysterious that it had, like an algebra equation, an "X" for which the author needed to solve:

Joseph Heller described the conception of *Catch-22* this way: "I was lying in bed when suddenly this line came to me: 'It was love at first sight. The first time he saw the chaplain X fell madly in love with him.'" The "X" turned out to be Yossarian, but Heller didn't have the name, didn't even know that this "X" was in the Army. "The chaplain wasn't necessarily an army chaplain," he said. "He could have been a prison chaplain. I don't understand the process of imagination though I know that I am very much at its mercy. The ideas come to me in the course of a controlled daydream, a directed reverie."[8]

In her journal, George Eliot—just starting to write fiction and concerned about her ability to move beyond "mere" description to dramatic narrative—recalled, "One morning as I was thinking what should be the subject of my first story, my thoughts merged themselves into a dreamy doze, and I imagined myself writing a story, of which the title was 'The Sad Fortunes of the Reverend Amos Barton.'"[9]

This notion of controlled daydream, directed reverie, or waking doze lies behind the "guided imagery" exercises that I sometimes use in my fiction-writing classes. Novelist Janet Beeler Shaw first introduced me to this technique. She learned it, in turn, from instructors at Illinois's Columbia College, who apparently rely heavily on this method. In one variation, a teacher asks students to close their eyes and imagine they're standing on the top stair leading to a basement they know well. Slowly, she guides them down the staircase, asking them at length to open their eyes and say what they "see" in the basement. After everyone has answered, the teacher instructs the students to close their eyes and imagine descending the stairs again. This time, she tells them to picture a person in the room, a person doing something, and when they next open their eyes, she has them write, as fast as they can, about what they see.

The exercise has endless permutations: a teacher asks students to imagine a long drive to an unfamiliar place, then to describe the first thing they see when they step out of the car; a teacher asks students to imagine themselves in a place of great darkness, then to describe the first light thing that strikes them; and so on.

What surprises me each time I do these exercises is the strength of the written responses and how favorably they compare to the pieces on which students spend time, the "at home" assignments.

The pedagogic notion of guided imagery is linked to what Joan Didion describes as the essential act of writing: "the process of thinking, of plugging into that electrical field of image and making an object out of the flash and the clatter."[10]

And how do you plug in? How do you open yourself up to worthwhile material and then select from it?

First, the clatter. It's not always easy to see, to be, as Henry James says, "one of the people on whom nothing is lost!"[11] In fact, it may be harder for us than it was for our predecessors. There's more clatter around. Or so it seems: an MTV world, ready to assault us, even as we devise ways to retreat.

And for young people, media garbage may be the biggest obstacle to writing truly. At the small Maine college where I teach, I have a student whose life has been nothing short of astounding. He is cheerful, energetic, gay, born-again Christian, and black. His mother was an addict. I believe she beat him. A few years ago, in the midwestern city he still calls home, his twin brother was murdered on his way home from a card game. At first, whenever this student wrote for me, he wrote soap operas—Danielle Steele fantasies of treachery and big business, luxurious cars, and perfectly attractive women.

"What do you do," people sometimes ask me, "with a student like that?" But it is only too obvious. I say: Tell your own story. This young man did, but only once, when he wrote about his brother, and then the story turned on the author's singing voice, a tenor that people tell me is achingly lovely.

I had this student in three consecutive classes. He wasn't shy about his life, and eventually his stories played themselves out in clubs or shared apartments or at drag pageants, but they retained that sense of a story borrowed from the media, of a tale as yet unmediated by life.

And why? Because the "public" or prevailing notion of story overwhelmed the private notion. Notions of entertainment got in the way of felt truth. When guided imagery exercises work, it's because students are thinking about life instead of art, what they've experienced instead of what they've read or "viewed." For some, this means abandoning the idea of Rambo as fiction, but even sophisticated students let their notions of story overwhelm them.

I had lunch recently with two women whom I'd met at a writing retreat. They're both quite accomplished and intelligent: one is a literature professor, the other a public relations specialist. Over the course of the weekend, both had written wonderful short exercises for me. In talking about why they'd written so little in the months since then, the literature professor said, "Oh, I have plenty of ideas. I just don't know how to make them into stories." The public relations specialist nodded her head: That was exactly *her* problem: she had characters and situations but nothing else. There was a silence, and then she said to the professor, "I always remember that exercise *you* wrote, about the woman walking across the street." I smiled. I remembered it, too. It had been a striking piece, about a young woman hurrying across a Paris boulevard to go . . . somewhere; the piece never got that far. "But what am I to do with it?" the professor said. We'd all become friends, so I felt strange playing teacher, still I felt I should offer something. What I came up with sounded insufficient, obnoxiously breezy even, but it was my honest answer: "Just have her go somewhere the next street over, and when she gets there, have something happen."

I think in this regard of Jane Smiley, who said that her short story "Lily" came about when she imagined what would happen if some friends of hers—a couple and a woman who didn't know each other—were to meet.[12] Though I don't know how Smiley composed "Lily," I can guess at her process. She already had her characters, so she didn't need to start with that. Instead, she had to imagine an occasion for bringing the couple and the woman together. The three could have met at a restaurant or on a ship or in an adult ed class, but as Smiley set it up, the couple ended up being guests in the house of a woman named Lily. And, then, of course, there needed to be a reason why the couple was visiting Lily, a reason they knew her, a reason they were coming to say hello; there needed to be a past history and a current situation.

To think of all this isn't to think about story as much as character and situation, the very thing that the professor and public relations specialist already knew how to do. To develop their stories, my former students had only to do what Turgenev did with his hovering visions; they had only, in Henry James's words, "to imagine, to invent and select and piece together the situations most useful and favorable to the sense of the creatures themselves, the complications they would be most likely to produce and feel."[13] They had only to do what they were already doing . . . and forget about story.

BUT I'M making it sound easier than it is. I know that. Still, there are ways to help oneself out. Patricia Henley asks her students to take long walks before they write. The idea, she says, is to get them in a contemplative mood, to let motion induce thought, to get "junk stories" out of their heads so their own stories can emerge.

Others have less healthy methods of making this happen. There's a reason alcohol is an occupational hazard for writers. It's a way—among ways—to access material. (Think of Coleridge, who dreamed the better part of "Kubla Khan" after taking opium.) But it's probably less true that drugs "give" one material than that they release inhibitions, allowing (some) writers to ignore the part of themselves that dismisses a trigger before it has a chance to develop. Back to my professor friend: if she had allowed her character to finish crossing the street, and if she had abandoned the question of whether her piece did or did not have a strong narrative, her imagination might have taken care of the rest. The painter Philip Guston once said, "If the artist starts evaluating himself, it's an enormous block, isn't it?"[14] And of course it is. At the very least, to "plug into the electrical field of image," one needs to shut one's censor down, to give the creative self a chance.

Of course, "plugging in" is only the first problem. Plugging in may open us to something like Turgenev's hovering visions, but it leaves us where my professor friend was left: with the problem of selection. Once we've plugged in, what will we pick to address? What will we make happen? In "The Death of Justina," John Cheever writes, "Fiction is art and art is the triumph over chaos (no less) and we can accomplish this only by the most vigilant exercise of choice, but in a world that changes more swiftly than we can perceive there is always the danger that our powers of selection will be mistaken and that the vision we serve will come to nothing."[15] This notion of choice has its parallels in the other arts. You choose to paint the peaches and not the landscape. You sculpt the bust and not the torso. You can't do the whole world; you can't do all your perceptions; you have to pick. But what should your criteria for selection be? Cheever complains, directly or obliquely, in almost all the stories in his *Some People, Places, and Things That Will Not Appear in My Next Novel* about the mutability of values that makes it so hard to decide what we *should* write about. How, he wants to know, would Gogol or Thackeray write about a suburban bomb shelter decorated with composition gnomes?

There's a famous story about Chekhov telling a visitor that one could write a story about anything. "Do you know how I write my stories? Here!" He picked up an ashtray lying nearby—presumably it was the first object he saw—and then said, "If you like, it will be a story tomorrow. . . . 'The Ashtray.'"[16]

And what, I wonder, would Chekhov do if he were sitting in my chair? The first object he'd see would be a "trophy treat," a plastic Michael Jordan head filled with gumballs. What with that? The problem here isn't junk stories borrowed from the media, but junk, the junk of life. In contemporary society, so much that is worthless claims our attention. And then we don't always know how to evaluate what we do see. Perhaps our confusion is the best we can do. Perhaps our confusion will have to be our subject.

IN HIS essay "Getting Started," John Irving writes, "Here is a useful rule for beginning: Know the story—as much of the story as you can possibly know, if not the whole story—before you commit yourself to the first paragraph."[17] Irving has written far more novels than I will ever write. Clearly he knows what works for himself in a way that I don't for myself, but this seems like terrible advice. I'm more inclined to E. L. Doctorow's wisdom. He said that writing a novel is like driving at night. You don't need to see the whole road, just the bit of illuminated blacktop before you.[18]

It's true that you wouldn't tell a story at a party unless you knew the whole story start to finish. Presumably, only children and hopeless bores say, "Oh, listen to this," and then ramble until something comes to them. But that doesn't mean Irving's advice is good. There are more parallels between party anecdotes and publishing, the final stage of writing, than with the beginning stages of writing. That's why we don't publish our first drafts, why we wait a long time before we say, "Oh, listen to this."

William Faulkner didn't know his whole story before he put pen to paper. "The stories with me," he once said in an interview, "begin with an anecdote or a sentence or an expression, and I'll start from there, and sometimes I write the thing backwards—I myself don't know exactly where any story is going."[19]

Even if you decide, with Irving, that you must know the road before you travel, you may not end up where you intended. That's why writers say that writing is discovery. And mean it. And that's why a trigger can be buried in a story or so transformed that no one, save the author, could ever guess at a story's source.

Joan Didion writes that the woman in the white halter dress, the one who inspired *Play It as It Lays*, "appears in the novel, only obliquely, in a chapter which begins: 'Maria made a list of things she would never do. She would never: walk through the Sands or Caesar's alone after midnight. She would never: ball at a party, do S-M unless she wanted to, borrow furs from Ben Lipsey, deal.'"[20]

Another example: When the father of a friend of writer Amy

Godine came out of the closet, his community vilified him. But the daughter, Godine's friend, decided to return home from college to say that *she* accepted who he was. But when she returned home, she found two young men smoking pot in front of the living room TV. Instead of embracing her father, Godine's friend sat down and got high with the visitors. Godine says, "I never got over the image of coming home to say, 'Dad, I love you,' and there were these street toughs—it was so heartbreaking and funny."[21]

Heartbreaking and funny. Fiction fodder. Godine decided to tell the story as she knew it: from her friend's point of view. But that didn't work. In the end, the story Godine *did* write—"The Gardener," which appeared in the *North American Review*—was told from the point of view of one of the father's lovers, a man who, in fictional garb, became the house gardener.

For both Godine and Didion, the trigger anecdotes (about the friend returning home or the woman walking across the casino) have a point, a certain emotional resonance about disappointed expectations or dissipated glamour. Godine and Didion's stories, though, ended up lying elsewhere: in the unknown aspects of the anecdote, in the questions that party guests might ask (if they dared) after the telling. "OK, OK, but what I still don't *get* . . ."

IF MOST fiction is a mixture of experience and invention, then one way to trigger a story may be to self-consciously lead yourself to invention through experience. "I never travel without my diary," says a character in Oscar Wilde's *The Importance of Being Earnest*. "One should always have something sensational to read in the train."[22] Of course, not everyone's so smitten with his or her own life. For those who are not, there's Rainer Maria Rilke's reprimand in *Letters to a Young Poet:* "If your everyday life seems poor, don't blame *it;* blame yourself; admit to yourself that you are not enough of a poet to call forth its riches."[23]

To get her students writing, author Elizabeth Searle asks them to start a page with the words "I remember." She instructs them to write for as long as possible, and when they can think of nothing else to say, they write, "I remember" again. Short story writer Lisa Ruffolo has her students do "memory maps." They draw the floor plans of the houses or apartments they grew up in, then put a memory in each room—not a description but a specific memory of something that took place there. A more sophisticated variant of this appears in Pamela Painter and Anne Bernays's helpful book, *What If? Writing Exercises for Fiction Writers*. In "Family Stories, Family Myths," an exercise from Katherine Haake, student writers start by selecting an oft-told family story. Assuming the persona of one of the participants in the story, the student writer composes a letter to another family member, explaining the "truth" of what happened. Then the students trade letters and respond by taking the persona of the addressee of the original letter. (I can almost imagine Eudora Welty's famous story "Why I Live at the P.O." as a response to this assignment.)

The purpose of all these exercises is to help identify what matters to you and, in the process, to stumble across a story idea. Good exercises don't ask you to be clever or go hunting for the meaningful. After all, if you *begin* thinking in terms of what is and isn't important to write about, the "emotionally and intellectually significant" (which, John Gardner held, you *must* address), you'll undoubtedly veer off track. It's probably best to look for triggers in what genuinely interests you . . . and trust the universality of your particular concerns.

In advising a young writer, F. Scott Fitzgerald once said, "You've got to sell your heart, your strongest reactions, not the little minor things that only touch you lightly, the little experiences that you might tell at dinner. This is especially true when you *begin* to write, when you have not developed the tricks of interesting people on paper, when you have none of the technique which it takes time to learn. When, in short, you have *only* your emotions to sell."[24] Note: His emphasis isn't on what's important but on what's important to *you,* what attracts or compels *you.* Your problems with food? Your father's death? You could be Jenefer Shute and write *Life-Size* or James Agee and write *A Death in the Family.* You could exploit your anxiety about environmental disaster or your general feelings of failure. (Think of Don DeLillo's *White Noise* or Saul Bellow's *Seize the Day.*)

It needn't be personal history, though. Your "strongest reaction" could come from song lyrics. (One of my favorite student stories was inspired by a Tom Waits line.) It could come from an overheard bit of conversation (eavesdropping, a time-honored literary tool). It could come from a peculiar experience. (Jill McCorkle was just starting a new novel when she happened to dig up a high-top sneaker in her garden. The find unnerved her. "What if," she thought, "there's a foot attached?"[25] And so, in the novel *Carolina Moon*, a woman gets a delivery of topsoil, and there *is* a body in it.) It could come from a story you heard years ago. (Paging through a worn volume from a secondhand shop, Joseph Conrad stumbled across an anecdote about a silver thief. He'd originally heard the story, decades earlier, when he was sailing in the Gulf of Mexico. The anecdote itself didn't spark his imagination—there was nothing much to it—but the recollection did, for it made him reminisce about his seafaring youth when, as he writes in "Preface to *Nostromo*," "Everything was so fresh, so surprising, so venturesome, so interesting; bits of strange coasts under the stars, shadows of hills in the sunshine, men's passions in the dusk, gossip half forgotten, faces grown dim." And all this made him feel that "Perhaps, perhaps, there still was in the world something to write about.")[26]

And finally, though I've hardly exhausted the alternatives, your strongest reaction could come from a dispiriting outing. What's bad for life, after all, is often good for fiction.

I went once with Lorrie Moore and a group of other fiction writers to the Cave of the Mounds, a rather tacky tourist spot in Wisconsin. We were a group of women that day, all of us either single and unhappily so or toting boyfriends whom we would abandon within the year. There were exceptions. Lorrie may have been an exception. There may have even been a happily married couple along, but my sense of that day—and it may have been a projection of my own situation at the time—was of a shameful female irritation that there weren't any good guys around. I don't remember much about the cave, save that the walls were creepily veined and that the tour guide turned off the lights so we could experience the complete darkness of the cave. When the lights were flicked on, there was Lorrie, taking notes. *Notes!* I thought. *What could she find here?*

I do remember some other things about the day: some rock-shaped candies that I bought in the gift shop, but mostly the ride home. A doe ran out of the woods and darted up a highway embankment. Two others followed. This seemed strange, seeing so many deer up close. Then I realized: they were terrified. We passed by a suburban house with a deer up in a tree, blood draining onto the front lawn, and everything snapped into place. Orange vests started appearing. It was the first day of hunting season.

Two years later I opened up the *New Yorker* and read Lorrie Moore's funny, sorrowful story "The Jewish Hunter," which takes place partially at the fictitious Cave of the Many Mounds in Minneapolis. I felt excited, the way one does when one is party to another's romance or sees a setup working at a dinner. Why, I had been there! Had seen the initial sparks! And I felt something else, too: jealousy. Sure, we'd all met the guy, but only one of us had the skill to fall in love.

Getting In and Getting Out

FIRST WORDS ON FIRST (AND LAST) WORDS

FIRST MEMORIES, last words. When my sister was dying, we all told each other our first memories. Who knows why? I was the one who instigated it. I made everyone in the hospital room tell their stories. I offered my sister's, since I happened to know it and she had already spoken her last words. Her memory was of throwing a pair of maracas on the floor and being surprised to see beans spill out. So *that* was what made the sound. The memory that most startled me—perhaps because it replicated my current situation, beginning and ending in the same moment, the family crowded around the bed of the dying—was my grandmother's. Her first memory was of trying to stick her head between the many adult legs that surrounded her younger sister's crib, of reaching up to pull a toy from the blankets. But she was scolded away, for the baby was dead. I hadn't known till that moment that my grandmother had had a younger sister.

Of course we are alive before our first memories, and we survive, often enough, for a while past our last words. But even for the non-literary type, these markers seem like life's bookends, undeniably significant.

And as it is with life, so it is with fiction. We expect a lot from our openings and closings, more than from the rest of the lines we write. One might ask why. Why should firsts and lasts matter more than everything in the middle? Of course, this is an easier question to answer for fiction than for life. The opening is what entices a reader into a work. It doesn't matter how great the middle and end are if the reader never gets there, and the end is what the reader is left with, an impression of the whole that, ideally, resonates long after the book is closed.

A writer friend tells me that she once read that closings stick in a reader's short-term memory and that openings stick in a reader's long-term memory. I'm not sure what this means for the overall experience of a story, but invert the wisdom, and I'm reminded that all *my* real lessons about writing came from my elders and were about cocktail parties. Rule number one: It's always nice to make a good first impression, to handle yourself well for the short term of the evening. Rule number two: It's always nice to depart before you make an ass of yourself, to leave a favorable long-term impression.

AND EVEN these rules chafe. What rules don't when it comes to writing? We're all more or less mystics about what works and what doesn't and how to do what it is we do. That said, there are some generalizations one can make about openings and closings, a few eminently breakable rules that—when considered in light of specific examples—might serve as inspiration to those struggling to start or finish their work.

BUT, FIRST, a story about something that helped me in my thinking about beginnings and writing.

When I was in graduate school, I had a friend, Michelle, whose job it was to screen manuscripts for the Iowa Short Fiction prize. At the time, I had a job ghostwriting health textbooks for junior high school students. While I was busily typing up paragraphs on the dangers of smoking, she was lying on her bed and reading book after book of stories. Of course I was jealous. I thought reading stories and getting paid for it was just my kind of job . . . and yet it was hers. When I was with Michelle, I liked to tell her how lucky she was to be snuggling up to all that fiction.

"No, no, no," she told me on more than one occasion. "It's not what you think it is, Debra. If I have to read one more story that begins, 'The alarm clock rang,' I'll shoot myself."

"Oh, come on," I said. Michelle was given to hyperbole.

"No, seriously," she insisted. Half the stories she read started this way.

I don't know that I would have thought of this conversation again if not for the fact that I finally got a job I wanted. In my second year of graduate school, I taught a fiction-writing class. One evening, early in the semester, I went home, all eager to read my first batch of student papers. (At last, I was on the enviable side of the grading pen!) I turned to the first story and, sure enough, there, at the top of the page, were the words, "The alarm clock rang."

Of course, I laughed.

Just as I laughed the other day when I asked Don Lee, the editor of *Ploughshares,* if he had any advice about openings to stories. "Oh, you know," he said, somewhat tiredly. "No sunlight through the window. No alarm clocks. No transit stories about meeting stupid people on the bus. No hangovers."

Apparently, not much has changed in the fiction world since I was a graduate student. Back then, though, when I was a novice teacher, I wanted to understand why the alarm clock opening was so ubiquitous. Why would so many people start a story with this particular cliché? The answer was fairly obvious. If you don't know when your story begins, you simply start at the beginning of the *day* of the story. Better, of course, to start with the story itself. I wrote a note to my student, something to this effect, and turned to the next paper.

But later I thought about some of the stories I've most loved, and I realized that many don't start when the story begins any more than they start at daybreak. Instead, they begin in the middle, after a great deal of action has already taken place.

I asked my friend, writer Steve Stern, if he had anything smart to say about how a story opens, and he sighed, presumably at the paucity of his knowledge, and said, "Well, only that old bromide. You know, how the story has to be in motion when you start and then you can sneak around to the back door and fill in with whatever expository material you need."

Now, plenty of good stories *don't* start in the middle of things, but ever since Horace, this "begin in the middle" advice has been a mainstay of writerly wisdom. Alice Munro adheres to it when she opens "Miles City, Montana," with the line, "My father came across the field carrying the body of the boy who had been drowned."[1] Clearly, this is an *in medias res* opening, since before the story even starts, a boy has been drowned and the narrator's father has gone to retrieve the body. Part of our expectation for a good story has to do with how much has already happened. There's so much to be explained: we're interested in all the expository material that is going to be introduced through the back door. But we're interested in the future as well. If this much has already happened, if we already have a drowned boy and a father retrieving that boy, what could possibly be next? The opening sentence of Andre Dubus's "Townies" does the same thing. "The campus security guard found her" makes you think, "My God! What happened to her that she needed to be found?"[2]

AS STORYTELLERS, we imagine the best question we can be asked is, "And then what? What happened next?" In this way, we're all closet Scheherazades. But we're also all would-be analysts—and nosy ones at that. We want to know what happened before, what in the past explains what is before us in the present. Consider the opening of Cynthia Ozick's "Rosa": "Rosa Lublin, a madwoman and a scavenger, gave up her store—she smashed it up herself—and moved to Miami."[3]

Madwoman, scavenger. What's happened that Rosa is characterized this way? And *smashed it up herself.* What's *that* all about? The *in medias res* opening appeals to our gossipy selves. It makes us ask snooping questions, and it promises answers . . . if we'll only read on.

But what makes Ozick's opening effective is more than its *in medias res* status. The authority of the writing, the intensity of the information, and the very queerness of the details intrigue.

And, of course, one of the bad things about "the alarm clock rang" opening is that it's boring, overly familiar. No surprise, then, that many openings succeed by opting for the *un*familiar, if only for a moment. Writer Eberle Umbach has a story that starts, "The flesh opened in pink folds."[4] She's describing the carving of a ham, but at first you don't know that. You jump at the image, then check the cover of your high-minded literary magazine. A metamorphosis? When did it turn into *Playboy?*

Writer Elizabeth Searle notes that a lot of fine openings have the virtue of the carving-a-ham line: they make you think, "Wait. That can't be right."[5] They offer a moment of confusion that is interesting rather than discouraging.

Stuart Dybek opens "Hot Ice" by writing, "The saint, a virgin, was uncorrupted. She had been frozen in a block of ice many years ago."[6] And Louise Erdrich begins "Saint Marie" by saying, "So when I went there, I knew the dark fish must rise."[7] Your second reaction to these lines may be, "Oh, intriguing image," but your first, your immediate, reaction is probably, "Huh?"

The first words of Robert Olen Butler's "A Good Scent from a

Strange Mountain" certainly are a puzzle: "Ho Chi Minh came to me again last night, his hands covered with confectioners' sugar."[8] How can you *not* love that? The wild image of the famed leader with sugar on his hands, so ordinary a detail is almost magical in this context. And what a strange sentence. He "came to me." Well, who are you? And what do you mean that he "came" to you? And then there's that small word *again*. This, too, is a "middle of things" story, for apparently Ho Chi Minh has been visiting regularly. This story has a history with . . . well . . . History. And finally there are the words *last night*. That's the kind of small phrase that orients the reader, economically and effectively. The "now" of the story is "this morning," the morning after "last night," and the speaker is ready to tell us all about it.

An apparent contradiction in an opening is often the thing that puzzles us enough to read on. Steve Stern opens his story "Lazar Malkin Enters Heaven" by writing, "My father-in-law, Lazar Malkin, may he rest in peace, refused to die."[9] Why is the narrator saying "may he rest in peace" about a person who won't die? And what, anyway, does it mean to "refuse" death?

Hemingway begins "The Snows of Kilimanjaro" by writing, "'The marvellous thing is that it's painless,' he said. 'That's how you know when it starts.'"[10]

Well, that makes no sense, of course. How can an absence of a feeling signal you to the start of something? And what does that pronoun *it* refer to? What could Hemingway possibly be talking about?

OFTEN ENOUGH, slightly curious sentences deliver an image or line so fantastic that we feel the promise of a good story ahead. That same sense of promise can be given in a line that isn't initially confusing, can be given because a character is so startling or insistent or passionately presented that we can't help but want to stay with him or her. Consider Mona Simpson's short story "Lawns." The story begins with two easy-to-understand words: "I steal."[11]

"My God," says writer Jessica Treadway of this opening sentence, "who *wouldn't* want to read on?"[12] What could be next? And what can we expect of the kind of a person who would say something like this about herself? Say it, in fact, before she lets us know anything else about her?

And what can we expect of the self-conscious narrator of James Alan McPherson's "The Story of a Scar"?

Since Dr. Wayland was late and there were no recent news-magazines in the waiting room, I turned to the other patient and said: "As a concerned person, and as your brother, I ask you, without meaning to offend, how did you get that scar on the side of your face?"

The woman seemed insulted. Her brown eyes, which before had been wandering vacuously around the room, narrowed suddenly and sparked humbling reprimands at me.[13]

With the McPherson opening, the very energy of the telling is as much a goad to further reading as the prickly relationship established in the second paragraph and the sense that there's an interesting story about the characters' respective injuries.

And here we're back to my cocktail party theory of writing, which is that the pretzels can be stale, the wine can be Mad Dog, but you've still got a good gathering if the energy is right. Honest, unforced emotion of any stripe is always interesting and immediate emotion, as much as anything else, plunges us into a story.

"Joel," Margaret Atwood writes at the opening of her story "Ugly-puss," "hates November. As far as he's concerned they could drop it down the chute and he wouldn't complain. Drizzle and chill, everyone depressed, and then the winter to go through afterwards. The landlord had turned down the heat again, which means Joel has to either let his buns solidify and break off or use the electric heater, which means more money, because the electricity's extra. The land-lord does this to spite him, Joel, personally. Just for that, Joel refuses to move."[14]

Already Joel sounds like an Uglypuss himself, but we don't need to like Joel to be engaged in his thoughts. Indeed, we may feel, right away, that he's going to teach us something about the inner life of a crank like him, and the way in which the narrator adopts Joel's manner of speech—"drop it down the chute," "let his buns solidify and break off"—makes the story feel as "in your face" as we must imagine Joel is.

Beyond this advice about beginning in the middle, intriguing with momentary confusion, and aiming for passion, what else can we say about openings? We can observe that sometimes the world really does bead itself in a drop of dew, that the germ of the whole story may be in the initial part.

Rust Hills, the former fiction editor of *Esquire* and the author of *Writing in General and the Short Story in Particular,* claims that, "What the beginning of a short story *should* do, what the beginnings of most successful modern short stories usually do, is begin to state the *theme* of the story right from the very first line."[15]

Now to judge how well a beginning does this, you'd have to read the whole story, but I think you can get an *idea* of theme from the first line of a story like David Quammen's "Walking Out": "As the train rocked dead at Livingston he saw the man, in a worn khaki shirt with button flaps buttoned, arms crossed."[16]

What you can guess here about "theme" is that there's something significant about the tight way the man is holding himself, that the phrase "rocked dead" has some import, and that it makes a difference that this is a train coming in, since we know the title of the story is "Walking Out."

You can also get an idea of theme from the first line of Bernard Malamud's "The Last Mohican": "Fidelman, a self-confessed failure as a painter, came to Italy to prepare a critical study of Giotto, the opening chapter of which he had carried across the ocean in a new pigskin-leather briefcase, now gripped in his perspiring hand."[17]

The ironies here are a clue to what the writer is eventually going to touch on. We can presume that Fidelman is the name of a Jew, so what's he doing with a "pigskin-leather briefcase"? That's hardly kosher. Clearly, his relationship to his own tradition is a bit shaky. Or really more than a bit shaky because his chosen subject of study is Giotto, the great Christian painter, a subject with which Fidelman (presumably) doesn't have a pure relationship, an honest feeling. And what do we make of the fact that Fidelman is that academic cliché, the failed artist who becomes a critic? The story ends with a poor Jew quoting Tolstoy and asking, "Why is art?" The answer, the revelation that Fidelman has in the final moments of the story, is that art, as Tolstoy says, is the means of transferring feeling from one man's heart to another, and, for the first time, Fidelman understands why his Giotto project is so very misguided.

Theme in Malamud is clearly stated from the very first line, but I don't think that you should, therefore, use Hills's advice as a rule but as a potential source of inspiration. Theme, as Flannery O'Connor has said, isn't something you can simply "add" to your story, like calcium to orange juice, to make it better. But a first line can, as writer

Elizabeth Searle says, be like a seed, a whole story can come out of it. Sometimes, once you have found the right first line, you've found your story.

The title story of Searle's collection *My Body to You* starts with the line, "Above me, a boy is trying to guess my sex."[18]

The scene she is describing takes place in the subway. The speaker is seated, "the boy" hanging on a pole by her. Now there's definitely something off in that line. It *does* seem to be the opening to a story that's starting in the middle of things. Elizabeth says that the sentence helped her discover what her story was about. From the start, she had the line, "A boy is trying to guess my sex," but things didn't take off till she added the words "above me." And even then, she spent a lot of time shifting things around, trying to figure out where to put that new phrase.

> A boy above me is trying to guess my sex.
> OK, but the first half of the sentence seems less strong than the second half.
> A boy is trying to guess my sex above me.
> Not grammatical. What's that "above me" supposed to modify?
> Above me, a boy is trying to guess my sex.

All that time spent shifting the phrase around helped Searle figure out that the story she was writing was about her female narrator and the position of that woman's body in relation to others. So in the end, her first line helped her discover her story, discover its theme and some of its content, which is a lot of good work for one sentence.

FOR MANY writers, closings are harder to do than openings, the difference between potential and realized potential. At the start of life, "Da-da" and "Ma-ma" is an accomplishment, and simply to have a first memory is valuable; we don't expect ourselves to have a *significant* first memory. But we do expect something out of last words, something that will make the life that is lapsing, as well as life in general, less of a mystery. We want, in short, our ends to have meaning, or, if that sounds too grand, we want our endings to make some sense of what has come before. The convention is that a closing will tie together the body of the story by offering an image or thought or final piece of information that gives one last, perspective-enhancing look on what has just happened.

In his letters, Anton Chekhov wrote, "My instinct tells me that at the end of a story or a novel, I must artfully concentrate for the reader an impression of the entire work, and therefore must casually mention something about those whom I have already presented. Perhaps I am in error."[19]

Now this modest statement came from a man who held that fiction needn't answer questions, only pose them, from a man who gave his characters, as Grace Paley might say, "the open destiny of life."[20] Indeed, Nabokov noted that a Chekhov story "does not really end, for as long as people are alive, there is no possible and definite conclusion to their troubles or hopes or dreams."[21]

All this would seem to make closure less of a problem. The story needs only an "impression," not an unnatural resolution, not a gravity-defying epiphany. What's more, the end doesn't need to be The End.

But it's more complicated than that, for Chekhov specified that the impression is to be "of the entire work."

In *Writing in General and the Short Story in Particular,* Rust Hills insists that one of the two requirements for short fiction is that the whole fit to the part and that the part fit to the whole. Till you get to the end of a story, the jury is essentially out on whether the piece has satisfied this requirement, which puts a fair amount of pressure on the end to do what (conceivably) the story itself has yet to do. As a less compressed form, novels aren't under as much pressure when it comes to the close, though I'm not quite sure I'd go as far as writer Josip Novakavich, who contends, "With novels, while it's essential to resolve the conflicts you raise, frequently the last page does not matter much—it is a kind of exit two-step jig."[22]

I thought I'd make the point about the pressures on an ending, particularly the pressures to answer for the body of the story, by describing an accomplished story that I don't like: T. Coraghessan Boyle's "Killing Babies," which appeared in the December 2, 1996, issue of the *New Yorker.* I always struggle when I think about Boyle's work, because he is an undeniable talent: a dazzling wordsmith, a fine satirist, an engaging, playful storyteller. Yet his work, though it entertains me in the beginning and middle, often irritates me in the end. "Killing Babies" is a perfect example of this; it's a reconfigured Cain and Abel story. The bad brother is Rick, recently out of rehab and staying with his "good" brother, Philip, a physician who lives with his wife and two children outside of Detroit. Both men veer toward clichés: Rick is the misbehaving addict whose ease at dismissing things doesn't mean he has a better idea about how to live his life, and Philip is your classic, uptight suburbanite. His face—we are told—is "trenched with anal retentive misery." But Philip happens to work at an abortion clinic—perhaps the good doctor is not so conventional after all?

Early in his stay with Philip, Rick learns that Philip's clinic and home are targets for right-wing anti-abortion protesters. When Philip takes his addict brother with him to work, Rick is enraged but also clearly excited by the fatuousness he sees in the protesters and by the nobility he imagines he sees in Sally, a young woman who forces herself through the crowd, presumably for an abortion.

As the story proceeds, Rick's anger at the protesters and his interest in Sally, whom he has glimpsed only once, grow out of control. Rick says that the young woman's look was "so poignant and so everlastingly sad I knew I'd never have another moment's rest till I took hold of it." Finally, Rick—high on whatever drugs he's been able to steal from his brother's supply closet—steps out of the clinic's front door and into a crowd of protesters, a group of fanatics draped over the building's entrance.

Rick concludes,

> The light was burning in my head, and it was all I needed. I reached into my pants and pulled out the gun. I could have anointed any one of them, but the woman was first. I bent to her where she lay on the unyielding concrete of the steps and touched that snub-nose to her ear as tenderly as any man of healing. The noise of it shut down Jesus, shut him down cold. Into the silence, and it was the hardware man next. Then I swung round on Mr. Beard.
> It was easy. It was nothing. Just like killing babies.

And so the story ends with a twist on the right wing view of things: abortion isn't murder, but murder is "merely" abortion. What is shooting people but killing babies? Adults, after all, are only babies with some years on them.

In Boyle's story, at the moment when, as a reader, you expect revelation or truth or something transcendent, you get just the opposite: no revelation, no truth. Instead, the story closes with a descendental, anti-ethical moment, which may be precisely T. C. Boyle's strategy; he's a postmodernist, resisting the modernist demand for meaning. But this is precisely why for all his prodigious talent, his stylistic skill, I find his stories so very frustrating. In the end, it feels he has nothing to say and believes there is nothing to say. Irony is an end in itself. That's the favorable reading of Boyle. The unfavorable one is that he doesn't know how to pull it off, that he doesn't know how to end his story—to resolve the intriguing complication of Sally, to finish the tale of the brothers—that if he could figure out something equal to all the great balls he's thrown up in the air, he'd catch them. Which is, I think, a clue to why endings are so hard for us. We don't know what to make of our own great material.

An unrelated example: years ago, I was in an undergraduate writing workshop. A man in the class handed in the first half of a story. No one had ever done this before—submitted an incomplete work—but we forgave him, for we were quite taken with the fragment we got. It was about a photographer—long unemployed, presumably because of a dark depression—who spends nights listening to the police radio. One night, a fire is reported and the man pulls himself out of his slump to go photograph it. When he develops his film, he discovers that every other shot on the contact sheet is Ansel Adams's famous photograph, "Moonrise over Hernandez."

"Cool," we all said to him. How would it turn out? We professed ourselves uniformly eager for the next installment. Which never came. The student writer slipped into his own malaise, writing nothing for the rest of the semester and, as far as I know, for the rest of his life. The student's curious idea about the contact sheet had done him in. He'd painted himself into a corner with his very skill. This is, I suppose, my criticism of Boyle's end. That he paints himself into a corner and then tries to jump over all that wet paint with a bit of outrageousness that shocks but doesn't satisfy.

All this means what? That we should paint in the other direction, to the easy escape route, the door? That we should be less wild and ambitious with our material? But this hardly seems like good advice. Perhaps endings simply require more patience than the other parts of a story. In speaking about endings, Elizabeth Searle says, "The end has to hit you." She means: the end is a matter of inspiration. It has to come to you. You can't fake it. It's like a title in that way; it is, more than other parts of the story, something that is less worked for than received. But, she adds, once you've been hit, you can write toward the end.[23]

Steve Stern echoes this piece of advice when he speaks of his own writing process. "I get the image that resolves a story before I get the story itself. Everything else is a retroactive process, a story that culminates in that image." He goes on to explain how this worked in his short story "Aaron Makes a Match."[24] He had the idea, he says, of "a boy whose aunt was dying and her soul was trying to escape from her body, and her body was hanging on, and I knew this kid would help the soul escape. That would be his gift to his aunt, but I didn't know why any of this was happening and what there was between the boy and his aunt that would make this gesture resolve whatever dynamic there was between them."[25]

TO LIST strategies for ending a story may be less helpful than it is for openings, since a list of strategies begs the larger question of inspiration, of how to understand your own story, of how to discover what you mean to say. That said, in general, when we think of effective closings, we think of a resonant final image or a powerful thought or a "killer" line. Or we think of some combination of these three.

John Cheever's "The Country Husband" ends in a suburban yard with this paragraph:

"Here, pussy, here, poor pussy!" But the cat gives her a skeptical look and stumbles away in its skirts. The last to come is Jupiter. He prances through the tomato vines, holding in his generous mouth the remains of an evening slipper. Then it is dark; it is a night where kings in golden suits ride elephants over the mountains.[26]

Who knows what that final image means? I sure don't, but I love it, love how suddenly porous my skin feels when I read it, love the sense that the world—this very world with its scavenging cats and workaday vegetation—opens and opens readily, easily, to contain this mysterious image.

A less puzzling but equally impressive final image comes from Amy Hempel's "In the Garden Where Al Jolson Is Buried." The narrator of this story goes to the hospital to visit her best friend. As close as the friends have been, the narrator has not come before, for she is unable to cope with her friend's terminal illness. What's more, during her single visit, the narrator tries to deflect emotion with humor and trivia. But this suits her friend just fine. Indeed, the story opens with the ill friend saying, "Tell me things I won't mind forgetting. Make it useless stuff or skip it."

So the narrator responds, "Did you know when they taught the first chimp to talk, it lied? When they asked her who did it on the desk, she signed back Max, the janitor."

The ill friend laughs but declines to hear more, since the narrator says the rest of the story "will break your heart."

Later, much later, at the story's conclusion, when the friend *has* died, the narrator finishes off the chimp story. First, though, the narrator confesses that, in her state of extreme grief, she can't think clearly. She remembers nothing—or she only remembers trivia, "things that she won't mind forgetting." Otherwise, nothing, nothing true, reaches her until she thinks of the chimp with the talking hands. And then Hempel concludes with this combination of image and thought:

> In the course of the experiment, the chimp had a baby. Imagine how her trainers must have been thrilled when the mother, without prompting, began to sign to the newborn. Baby, drink milk. Baby, play ball. And when the baby died, the mother stood over the body, her wrinkled hands moving with animal grace, forming again and again the words, Baby, come hug, Baby, come hug, fluent now in the language of grief.[27]

What the narrator had earlier promised is true; the chimp story does break our hearts. The conclusion ties the piece together. Till the end, everything in the story has been either a metaphor for injury or a bit of trivia, but the final bit of trivia embraces the very thing that the narrator cannot: her own terrible emotions. And as sad as the end is, it has, I think, some of the same largeness as the Cheever close. There's the same sense of the story opening up, in its final moments, to how enormous things are, in this case, how enormously painful.

Robert Olen Butler's "A Good Scent from a Strange Mountain" uses a resonant line and something like an olfactory image to achieve a similar effect. When "A Good Scent" opens, the story's Buddhist narrator is at the end of a long life and is being visited nightly by Ho Chi Minh's ghost. Years earlier, the narrator worked in a French pastry kitchen with Ho Chi Minh. Now, Ho Chi Minh's ghost is unable to rest because he cannot remember how to make a glaze, a recipe he learned in that pastry kitchen. Much else happens in this wonderful story—it's criminal for me to reduce it this way—but the piece finishes up with these words from the narrator:

> I know now what it is that he [Ho Chi Minh] has forgotten. He has used confectioners' sugar for his glaze fondant and he should be using granulated sugar. I was only a washer of dishes but I did listen carefully when Monsieur Escoffier spoke. I wanted to understand everything. His kitchen was full of such smells that you knew you had to understand everything or you would be incomplete forever.[28]

Perhaps the reason I so love this line is it says the opposite of what the T. C. Boyle "Killing Babies" close seems to say: "It all counts. Everything makes a difference. It's all important."

For this affirmation, the Butler story is, I think, as political as it is spiritual. Critic Jan Clausen says that political fiction is not fiction that elaborates, necessarily, on what's going on in Bosnia and the like, but fiction that reminds us that what happens to humans matters and matters desperately. Even endings that show people going on with their lives, virtually dismissing the story's main character, do this. When Kafka closes "Metamorphosis," Gregor isn't even in the picture. And here is the end of V. S. Naipaul's *A House for Mr. Biswas,* the lengthy depiction of a life in which Mr. Biswas's desire for a home becomes symbolic of his desire for an independent identity:

> The cremation, one of the few permitted by the Health Department, was conducted on the banks of a muddy stream and attracted spectators of various races. Afterwards the sisters returned to their respective homes and Shama and the children went back in the Prefect to the empty house.[29]

Both Kafka and Naipaul's final lines seem to declare the superfluity of the characters with whom we've been engaged. It's as if, with the endings, the narrator has said, as Carol Shields *does* say in the final line of her novel *The Stone Diaries,* "Ah, well."[30] But it's a dismissive expression we don't, as readers, share in, and that's part of its strength. We don't forget the ignored or forgotten. The large cockroach, mad Mr. Biswas—they stay with us. They make themselves matter and make us, as a result, matter, too.

"Bring stones," Harriet Doerr writes when she closes her novel *Stones for Ibarra,* and the command is directed toward memory.[31] Don't forget. This meant something. This all meant something.

And it doesn't matter that we can't quite articulate what that something is, for the best endings seem to be barely contained by the words in which they are expressed. They feel bigger than mere words; they practically transcend themselves on the page. And the words' ability to slip out of their own skins may have to do with accumulated meaning rather than beauty of expression. For example, Roddy Doyle's novel *Paddy Clarke Ha Ha Ha* ends with a relatively simple passage. Paddy Clarke's father—his da—has left his mother but has returned for a holiday visit. The concluding scene takes place at the door to the house:

> He saw me.
> —Patrick, he said.
> He moved the parcels he had with him under one arm and put his hand out.
> —How are you? he said.
> He put his hand out for me to shake it.
> —How are you?
> His hand felt cold and big, dry and hard.
> —Very well, thank you.[32]

I cried at that final line, and there's no accounting for my fat tears unless you've read the whole book and seen what a masterful portrayal of boyhood it is and seen how Paddy—a sharp, funny, curious, cruel but wonderfully observant and sensitive boy—has for himself only one wish: not to care about what happens around him, not to care about the fights between his ma and da, not to feel everything so profoundly. And it seems, horribly, with that formal final line to his father, that line that is such a lie, that Paddy has in fact been granted his desire. He's becoming hardened to the world. The story ends not with a revelation, exactly, but a transformation, a shift the reader can't welcome even if it feels inevitable.

And we see these transformations at the end of the best fiction. One variant of this transformation often appears at the close of coming of age stories, like James Joyce's "Araby," Frank O'Connor's "The Guests of the Nation," and John Updike's "A&P." In all these stories, the concluding transformation is violent and wrenching, and there is a frank acknowledgment of it as the story ends. "And anything that ever happened to me afterwards," says O'Connor's young Irish soldier-narrator, "I never felt the same about again."[33]

THE "LARGENESS" of so many final transformations is often accompanied by a startling intimacy, as if just before the illusion ends, the writer wants to remind readers that, by sheer virtue of being human, they participate in the conclusion. Certainly this is what seems to happen in the famous final paragraph of James Joyce's "The Dead":

> A few light taps upon the pane made him turn to the window. It had begun to snow again. He watched sleepily the flakes, silver and dark, falling obliquely toward the lamplight. The time had come for him to set out on his journey westward. Yes, the newspapers were right; snow was general all over Ireland. It was falling on every part of the dark central plain, on the treeless hills, falling upon the Bog of Allen and, farther westward, softly falling into the dark mutinous Shannon waves. It was falling, too, upon every part of the lonely churchyard on the hill where Michael Furey lay buried. It lay thickly drifted on the crooked crosses and headstones, on the spears of the little gate, on the barren thorns. His soul swooned slowly as he heard the snow falling faintly through the universe and faintly falling, like the descent of their last end, upon all the living and the dead.

In an essay about "The Dead," Mary Gordon analyzes the images in this final paragraph and notes how everything is distinctly separate but still subject to the general snow; then she concludes her thoughts with praise for Joyce's final line.

Consider the daring of Joyce's final repetitions and reversals: "falling faintly, faintly falling"—a pure triumph of pure sound, of language as music. No one has ever equaled it; it makes those who have come after him pause for a minute, in awed gratitude, in discouragement. How can any of us come up to it? Only, perhaps, humbly, indifferently, in its honor and its name, to try.

And he did it all when he was twenty-five. The bastard.[34]

A funny close for an essay, I think. And a wise one, for who would chide Mary Gordon for her professional jealousy? After all, it's unsettling to see someone getting the ending so right so early in a career.

And as it is with fiction, so it is with life. We want our beginnings and endings separated. We want—don't we?—the middle to have its chance.

Speaking of Style

I'D LIKE to write something about prose style, and I come to this desire not because of my explicit interest in thinking about style but my explicit disinterest. The English language happens to be the only instrument I play by ear. Why learn to read music at this late date? I'm not conscious of reading for style either. I read what I like, or so I think. "I don't analyze 'em, I just watch 'em," a man who married into my family once said when he caught us biological Sparks endlessly rehashing a film. "He said that? Oh, puh-leeze," his wife laughed when I related the conversation. As for my own anti-intellectual claim, it was recently put to the test. Last winter, I served as judge for a writing contest. I read so many stories that I stopped thinking in terms of how many manuscripts I had to read and started thinking in terms of weight. As in: how many pounds of fiction could I read during my son's nap time? I intended to abandon all weak efforts on page two, so it was with great horror that I discovered that almost all of the stories were well done. In the end, stylistic distinction tipped me (and my co-judge) in favor of one accomplished story over another. I'd think this was just the result of my aesthetic kinship with the other judge, but my most recent undergraduate writing class proved me wrong. For the semester, I ordered Jim Shepard and Ron Hansen's anthology, *You've Got to Read This: Contemporary Writers Introduce Stories That Held Them in Awe.* As the title suggests, the anthology consists of writers introducing stories they love, and I made my students do the same. Assignment: Find a story in a contemporary magazine or literary journal, present it to the class, then tell me (in an essay) why you love it. What distinguished the stories that the class picked wasn't (as I had anticipated it might be) a uniform content but stylistic uniqueness, an originality of expression that made the semester perhaps my happiest ever. I mean: I liked what my students assigned me to read.

And yet I've never really liked talking about style in class. I haven't had much to say. In fact, I always schedule my course's style discussion during winter, on a day when a blizzard might prevent me from making it to school. That way, I can show up post-storm, apologize for the missed class, acknowledge that style is important, then get to the next topic on the syllabus, something easier to articulate—a story's structure or the complexity of its characters.

My disinclination to develop my thoughts about style may be related to my vague idea—wrong, I know, but persistent nonetheless— that there's something embarrassing about talking about style, that it's like talking about ruffles, not the main garment; like enjoying a fashion magazine, indeed studying it, when one could be doing something worthwhile. Perhaps feeding the hungry? No one wants to be (as the poet James Galvin puts it) all polish and no car. One wants to write work that is substantial. And yet, clearly the subject of style is one that every writer (consciously or unconsciously) addresses. Even having little or no style is a kind of style.

I'LL BEGIN my maybe-morally-suspect-maybe-not discussion with the basics of prose style in fiction. I'll briefly identify the components of style, then move to the larger question of what style *is*, since knowing about the *parts* of style doesn't quite describe style or even answer the question of how a writer can *have* an individual style.

Normally when we talk about style, we mean the elements of language, though we quickly realize that these elements nudge into, if they don't overlap, areas like tone and voice. This is true of all parts of fiction; examining any one thing leads you into all things. Carefully consider the sentence "Lily, the caretaker's daughter, was literally run off her feet," and you've got a Ph.D. dissertation just waiting to happen.

That said, in *Three Genres: The Writing of Fiction, Poetry, and Drama,* Stephen Minot identifies four factors that determine prose style in fiction.[1]

First, diction or word choice. "Why 'explain,'" I remember my father once asking, in reference to a particularly pompous high school instructor of mine, "when you can 'explicate'?" The words we choose, the phrases we use—"dude" or "sir," "treatment modalities" or "plans," "blood clot in the diaper" or "this thing . . . like a tiny mouse heart packed in snow"[2]—mean everything. They suggest a level of formality, reveal or hide meaning, clarify or muddy images and emotions.

Second factor in prose style: syntax, or sentence structure. Do we write diffidently or garrulously? With unmodified subject-verb sentences or with fat, multiply modified complex-compound sentences? What patterns do we embrace or avoid? How do we create, or fail to create, unity, variety, and coherence?

Third factor, the balance of narrative modes, by which Minot means the balance between dialogue, thoughts, action, description, and exposition. Obviously, a story like Ernest Hemingway's "Hills Like White Elephants," which is largely dialogue, is stylistically different from an exposition-laden passage of Henry James's.

Fourth, verb tense. This is fairly self-explanatory—Minot mentions past and present tense, but we're also affected by the mood of verb tenses. Brief school days flashback: the mood of a verb can be indicative ("Her name is Jane"), imperative ("Watch out for Jane"), or subjunctive ("If it were Jane on the phone, we wouldn't be here today"). Certain stories—like Lorrie Moore's "How to Become a Writer" with its opening injunction to "First, try to be something, anything, else"—gain power by using, indeed emphasizing, nontraditional moods (largely imperative and subjunctive).[3]

TO MINOT's factors, we could add a few other things that are implied but not specifically identified in his list. Like figurative language. How often do we use it? How well? How imaginatively? Or mechanics. Punctuation can be crucial to how a piece works. Indeed, in the story "Guy de Maupassant," Isaac Babel—or to be more accurate, one of Isaac Babel's characters—puts the focus on diction and punctuation when he defines style. Having corrected a woman's dismal translation effort, Babel's narrator (half earnestly, half pompously) recalls his response to her admiring inquiry, "How did you do it?"

> I spoke to her of style, of an army of words, of the army in which every type of weapon is deployed. No iron spike can pierce a human heart as icily as a period in the right place.[4]

Babel isn't his character, isn't the young man of the narrative, and yet he clearly held his character's beliefs, for he was a famously obsessive reviser:

I go over each sentence, time and again. I start by cutting all the words it can do without. You have to keep your eye on the job because words are very sly, the rubbishy ones go into hiding and you have to dig them out. . . . A comparison must be as accurate as a slide rule, and as natural as the smell of fennel. Oh, I forgot—before I take out the rubbish, I break up the text into shorter sentences. The more full stops the better. I'd like to have that passed as a law. Not more than one idea and image to one sentence. . . . I take out all the participles and adverbs I can. . . . Only a genius can afford two adjectives to a noun. . . . Line is as important in prose as in an engraving. It has to be clear and hard.[5]

We're not mathematicians, however, and adding up factors—diction, syntax, balance of narrative modes, and verb tense—doesn't do justice to our "sense" of style. Even Babel's narrator in "Guy de Maupassant" gets more impressionistic when he tries to describe a specific writer's style. In complaining about the poor translation, Babel's narrator says, "The translation had no trace of Maupassant's free-flowing prose with its powerful breath of passion."[6]

When my undergraduate students and I describe a specific writer's style, we're similarly impressionistic but less poetic. We rarely get beyond the adjectives "straightforward" or "lyrical." "It really flows," someone may say. Or "It sounds conversational." After that, we're more or less stumped.

In her essay, "What We Talk About When We Talk About Style," Mary Stefaniak argues that graduate school writing students don't do much better. At least, in a classroom setting, they don't often look at how language functions, partially because they don't know how to. They don't have the vocabulary for such discussion, nor are their own stylistic decisions all that conscious.

In "Poetry and Grammar," Gertrude Stein writes, "When you are at school and learn grammar grammar is very exciting. I really do not know that anything has ever been more exciting than diagraming sentences. I suppose other things may be more exciting to others when they are at school but to me undoubtedly when I was at school the really completely exciting thing was diagraming sentences and that has been to me ever since the one thing that has been completely exciting and completely completing. I like the feeling the everlasting feeling of sentences as they diagram themselves."[7]

What seems funny about this isn't the pleasure in language, in how a sentence unfolds, in how syntax can be powerful, but the sense that the science of the matter is interesting. For most of us, it isn't. We don't really want to know how the piano is put together. We just want to be able to play it.

Of course, as Stefaniak notes, we needn't be grammarians to write effectively, though it might help when we *talk* about writing. It might give us a common language, but even so that common language would seem clinical, not right for what we're really interested in, which is the *effect* that a particular style has on us.

But Mary Stefaniak identifies one other reason why graduate-level writing classes fail to discuss style, and that is because most people, early in their writing lives, don't write distinctly.

And why not?

Because Stefaniak says, "Vision determines . . . style. Vision is hard to come by." Indeed, she argues, "The writer's vision determines what she will choose to write about, how much distance she will maintain between herself and the world of her fiction—and how close she will let the reader get to it—what words she will use and how she will arrange them into sentences to create her world on the page. Her 'style' reveals her stance toward the world; presents it rich in detail or laid bare, clean to the bone; puts rose—or blue or sepia—colored glasses on the reader or requires that we view the fictional world in gray or unequivocal black and white."[8]

As such, style is no ruffle on the garment; style is the garment itself. Style may be, as Jonathan Swift says, "Proper words in proper places,"[9] but his emphasis shouldn't mislead us into thinking style is "merely" about correctness, manners, and obedience to the rules. Style is essential. It is (again according to Stefaniak) *the writer's vision of the world made manifest* in the choice of words, the inclusion or exclusion of detail and metaphor, the structure of sentences."[10]

WHAT DOES this mean exactly? Stefaniak illustrates her definition with (among other things) this passage from the early Raymond

Carver story "Why Don't You Dance?" in *What We Talk about When We Talk about Love:*

> He lay down on the bed and put the pillow under his head.
> "How does it feel?" she said.
> "It feels fine," he said.
> She turned on her side and put her hands to his face.
> "Kiss me," she said.
> She closed her eyes. She held him.
> He said, "I'll see if anybody's home."[11]

How would we describe the style here? Stripped back. Minimalist, since that's the term that has been tossed around for a few decades. Meaning: we've got short choppy sentences, all in a standard subject-verb arrangement. Actually every phrase, outside dialogue, begins with *he* or *she.* There are no adjectives. The bed isn't squishy; the face isn't sunburnt. There are no adverbs. No "he lies down on the bed carefully." Indeed, there are no modifying phrases whatsoever. No lips rubbing against pillow covers, no small red line of pimples arcing, like a comma, around the corner of her mouth. Nothing.

Though Stefaniak doesn't explicitly say this, Raymond Carver has taken some standard advice on good writing—let verbs and nouns do the work in your sentence; limit adjectives and adverbs—to extremes. Norman Maclean, who taught composition for years before he wrote his mini-masterpiece, *A River Runs Through It,* says about writing: "Every little thing counts. You take the way it comes to you first, with adjectives and adverbs, and cut out all the crap. You use an adjective, it better be a sixty-four-dollar adjective. Turn off the faucet and let them come out one drop at a time."[12]

And yet, in Carver, there are no adjectives to be had at any price. The absence of modifiers prevents (as Stefaniak concludes) *any* sense of sensuality. We don't read Carver's prose simply as tight and well made. We read it as skeletal, stark, and disturbing.

And why aren't there any modifiers here? "Because," Stefaniak writes, "Carver's vision requires it. There are no nonrestrictive modifiers in Carver's prose here because there are no nonrestrictive details in his world. As Carver sees it, *all* details must restrict the meaning of an action. If they don't, they are not worth mentioning. More to the point, in Carver's fictional world, they do not exist. The girl's hand does not fall across her face because it is not necessary that it do so. It adds no shade of meaning—or, worse, the wrong shade of meaning. Such a detail *distracts* us from the austerity of the moment, from the brutal emptiness of human relationships as Carver sees them in this story."[13]

"Do not overwrite," advises Strunk and White's *The Elements of Style.* "Do not affect a breezy manner. . . . Be clear. . . . Place yourself in the background."[14] Doubtless Carver knows this. But *that's* not why he writes as he does. He writes the way he does because he sees the way he does.

LATER IN her essay, Stefaniak considers John Cheever, Carver's stylistic opposite, and still the maxim ("style is vision made manifest") holds true. For instance, here's the opening paragraph from "Goodbye, My Brother," Cheever's favorite of his own stories.

> We are a family that has always been very close in spirit. Our father was drowned in a sailing accident when we were young, and our mother has always stressed the fact that our familial relationships have a kind of permanence that we will never meet with again. I don't think about the family much, but when I remember its members and the coast where they lived and the sea salt that I think is in our blood, I am happy to recall that I am a Pommeroy—that I have the nose, the coloring, and the promise of longevity—and that while we are not a distinguished family, we enjoy the illusion, when we are together, that the Pommeroys are unique. I don't say any of this because I'm interested in family history or because this sense of uniqueness is deep or important to me but in order to advance the point that we are loyal to one another in spite of our differences, and that any rupture in this loyalty is a source of confusion and pain.[15]

There's a level of formality in the diction and tone here, one that contrasts with the apparently confessional nature of this introduction. Because the narrator is eager to appear precise, to seem to say exactly what he means, he stops to qualify and clarify his thoughts. The result is a medium length sentence followed by three multiply modified compound sentences. And even without reading further than this paragraph, we sense some comedy in the choice of words and the length of the sentences. There's nothing to distrust here exactly, and yet we suspect (despite the tone of reasonableness) that the resolution about the family is no resolution at all. And, indeed, we see that, perhaps in the early pun. The family is close "in spirit," the narrator says, referring to the colloquial meaning of that term, and yet he follows this conclusion with a sentence that starts (if read out of context) with a prayer ("Our father . . .") and forces the reader to take the "in spirit" literally. The narrator's father is dead; the closeness in the family indeed must be of the spirit.

"Goodbye, My Brother" is a latter day Cain and Abel story, one that culminates when the narrator strikes his irritatingly gloomy, puritanical brother, Lawrence, over the head with a piece of driftwood.

> Then I picked up a root and, coming at his back—although I have never hit a man from the back before—I swung the root, heavy with seawater behind me, and the momentum sped my arm and I gave him, my brother, a blow on the head that forced him to his knees on the sand, and I saw the blood come out and begin to darken his hair. Then I wished that he was dead, dead and about to be buried, not buried but about to be buried, because I did not want to be denied ceremony and decorum in putting him away, in putting him out of my consciousness, and I saw the rest of us—Chaddy and Mother and Diana and Helen—in mourning in the house on Belvedere Street that was torn down twenty years ago, greeting our guests and our relatives at the door and answering their mannerly condolences with our mannerly grief. Nothing decorous was lacking so that even if he had been murdered on a beach, one would feel before the tiresome ceremony ended that he had come into the winter of his life and that it was a law of nature, and a beautiful one, that Tifty should be buried in the cold, cold ground.[16]

The style here is as before, though intensified with rhythmic qualifiers, emphatic repetition ("cold, cold ground"; "dead, dead and about to be buried, not buried but about to be buried"), and counterintuitive adjectives (words like *mannerly* and *decorous* and *beautiful* in the aftermath of a murder).

In describing a completely different Cheever story, Stefaniak notes Cheever's use of modifier-heavy sentences, his discursive manner, his chunks of unbroken print. She concludes, "Here is a writer eager to interrupt himself, to pack more into the moment of the story, make it bigger, more important, resplendent with metaphor and cosmic implications."[17] For Cheever, everything counts, everything matters, everything is worth observing, and that's why his prose is so different from Carver's.

Indeed, we can easily imagine a Carver parody of Cheever:

> I hit my brother. There was blood on his face. I walked down the beach.

But the parody itself is unfair, because "Goodbye, My Brother" isn't a story Carver would have told, for his characters don't struggle with pain *and* pleasure, with how to enjoy life while well aware of hypocrisy, alcoholism, class tensions, the transitoriness of human existence, and so on. Carver would have been capable of rendering the bleakness of Cheever's world—the alcoholism, the sour nastiness of Tifty, the economic troubles—but not the pleasures and not the illusions of grandeur, and, in any case, Carver would have presented the troubles in an entirely different way. Or I should refine myself and say that "Goodbye, My Brother" is not a story that Carver could have told early in his life. As Raymond Carver got older, his life (by his own reckoning) happens to have improved (he got sober, he got out of an unhappy marriage into a happy one), and during the happy period of his life, his work changed.

William Faulkner once said, "The style—I think the story the writer is trying to tell invents, compels its style."[18] Certainly this was the case with Carver. At least, when he had stories that seemed open to the possibility of love and human connection (despite many similarities to his early work), his prose style grew more expansive.

For instance, his late story "A Small, Good Thing" is a longer, more detailed version of a story that was published early in his career as "The Bath." In revising the story for republication, Carver changed its meaning entirely. "The Bath" is a brief tale about human meanness. It has a ghostly, creepy feel. "A Small, Good Thing" is about grief and loss and the possibility of human connection, and one sees this in Carver's willingness to include details—indeed whole new scenes—that suggest the human effort to connect. The story itself is much longer than Carver's early stories, as are the individual sentences.

So: Carver and Cheever. Two very separate styles, two very separate visions. The men contrast neatly, but I could just as easily have made the same point with two other stylistic extremes—say, Ernest Hemingway and Henry James. After all, it makes sense that a person who once said, "Try to be one of the people on whom nothing is lost,"[19] would write as James did; that a man who suffered the world's limitations would write as Hemingway did.

I MENTIONED earlier that I recently served as a judge for a fiction-writing contest and that while reading, I despaired when I came across a well-done story, that I was looking for bad fiction to lighten my overall reading load. A terrible confession, isn't it? After all, I like to read. I love to read. But the source of my feelings is more complex than my own laziness. "Well done, well done, well done," I'd write in my public notes on the stories that I was judging, all the while thinking, "Shoot, shoot, shoot." I recognized the skill behind much of what I read, but I couldn't say I liked it. Not that I disliked it. It was well done. It was cooked. Nothing was runny, nothing was burnt . . . but well done feels like talent without vision. It's kind of a bore.

And there, I've said it. Well-done prose sucks. Give me something else. Give me something more.

"Life," a close writer friend of mine used to say, in a fake accent (Irish? Scottish? Russian? I never knew), "she eees so sad and beautiful." Which is basically my idea; life's sad and beautiful, and if you're half joking as you acknowledge it, that's all to the better. Life's strange, too. Like: the friend who used to say this, and who always struck me, for all her troubles, as so wise about life, so fun and irreverent, died due to a heroin addiction, died (directly? indirectly?) at her own hand. At any rate, I'm hardly original in my view of life. As a reader, I'm attracted to prose styles that embody this vision. Or, alternatively, embody a vision that I don't particularly share but astound me nonetheless.

What does this mean? I'll answer by way of example, using paragraphs from three of the stories that my most recent undergraduate class picked as "stories that held them in awe"—that is, from recently published stories that I (and at least one human being under twenty-two) really love.

THE NARRATOR of Aleksandar Hemon's "Passover" is (like the author) a Bosnian man trapped in the United States, "trapped" because he happened to be visiting the country when Sarajevo fell under siege. The story opens in 1994 Chicago with the narrator awake but in bed, "listening to the mizzle in [his] pillow, to the furniture furtively sagging, to the house creaking under wind assaults."[20] Later in the day, he has an interview for a job teaching English as a second language; the requirement of the interview pulls him from bed, though he's applied for work "strictly out of despair," having been laid off from his bookstore job.

"I closed the bathroom door," the narrator tells us in the story's second paragraph, "and the hooked towels trembled. There was the pungent smell of the plastic shower curtain and disintegrating soap. The toilet bowl was agape, with a dissolving piece of toilet paper in it throbbing like a jellyfish. The faucet was sternly counting off droplets. I took off my underwear and let it lie in a pile, then stepped behind the curtain and let the water run. Wee rainbows locked in bubbles streamed into the inevitable giddy whirl, as I fantasized about melting under the shower and disappearing into the drain."[21]

Even without the brief bit of background on the story and its author, this paragraph would surely strike us. The scene is familiar enough—man steps into a shower—but there's nothing ordinary about the language or, indeed, the intensity of perception, the apparently honest focus on the quotidian. The towels "trembled"; the toilet bowl is "agape"; the faucet doesn't drip, it sternly counts off droplets. The disintegrating toilet paper "throbs" like a jellyfish. The water, as it streams down, is "giddy." Hemon's diction anthropomorphizes his bathroom, but that's not all that's happening here. There's the oddly fey word *wee* for the rainbows and the sense of the whirl of water as "inevitable." In fact, the whirl of water *is* inevitable—that's what happens to water, it goes down the drain—but the use of the word *inevitable* instead of, say, *customary* adds a weight of meaning to this description. It undercuts the pleasure of the word *giddy* by introducing a curious note of fatalism into this description. These aren't good word choices, they're great, great because they pull one back, force one to see things that one would otherwise miss, and they do so while creating an appropriate emotional subtext for the story to come. The diction is both unusual and perfectly correct, a rather astounding achievement given that the narrator (and author) are relatively new to English. The obstacles to such fluency are brought home later in the story, when Hemon introduces Marcus, an ESL teacher whose "creative" use of language is invariably wrong. "Long time ago," Marcus says at one point, "I fell in love with a majestic, passionate woman, but fatuous circumstances took me elsewhere."

Hemon's bathroom description isn't simply a case of the author going through an ordinary description of a bathroom and having enough linguistic virtuosity to plug in a more interesting word. We wouldn't trust such a description, no matter how cleverly done; it would seem like mere artifice. The style here is intimately connected with the vision. It matters that Hemon's narrator notes things most of us would not—the pungent smell of curtain and soap; the look—instead of the feel—of the bathroom water. This is the writing of an outsider looking in. Hemon's language gives the bathroom a preternatural shimmer, because that's how the narrator—a man trapped by violence in the unfamiliar—experiences it. For him, the everyday *is* strange.

Two more sentences from early in the story:

Two white eggs roiled in the boiling water, like irisless eyes. The floor was sticky, so I had to unpeel my bare soles from the floor with every step—I thought of the movies in which people walk on the ceiling, upside down.

How imaginative, but how disturbing, to use a simile like "irisless eyes" for boiling eggs. How interesting, and how frightening, to speak of having to unpeel one's feet from the floor. Hemon notes all this because he can't not note it. Like Cheever, Hemon finds everything worth mentioning, though not because it matters exactly but because it has an impact, because it's what is present, instead of what used to be present.

Hemon's narrator observes language throughout "Passover." This fits with the ESL theme, but even before the ESL interview, the narrator notices the peculiar language of a LOST DOG poster, the curious names of the stores by which his bus passes (Inner Light Hair Sanctuary, Land of Submarines), and so on. Hemon is alive to language because it's not *his* language. His readers, in turn, are alive to language because Hemon uses it so unexpectedly. Words are part of Hemon's story. They're not just what he uses to tell his story; they're something to notice. It's impossible to avoid comparisons to Nabokov. Equally impossible not to think that Hemon's gifts are directly related to his troubles.

OF COURSE, I'd need to learn Serbo-Croatian and read Hemon's early stories to learn if my theory about stylistic distinction and the author's abrupt geographical displacement is true. In the end, the theory is not too useful for improving the prose of those of us who hope to avoid such a tragedy. But ruptures, of a different sort, between words and their referents, do account for the stylistic verve of the next passage I want to look at, the opening paragraph of George Saunders's short story "Jon."

> Back in the time of which I am speaking, due to our Coördinators had mandated us, we had all seen that educational video of "It's Yours to Do With What You Like!" in which teens like ourselfs speak on the healthy benefits of getting off by oneself and doing what one feels like in terms of self-touching, because love is a mystery but the mechanics of love need not be, so go off alone, see what is up, with you and your relation to your own gonads, and the main thing is, just have fun, feeling no shame![22]

How exactly to account for the expressive range of this inarticulate mix of clichés, this grab bag of euphemism, pop psych platitudes, educational mumbo jumbo, and pseudoinformation? Well, we're dealing with satire, obviously, and what's being satirized is the language of sex education but also (as is evident in the phrase "due to our Coördinators had mandated us") mind control. The speaker in this paragraph is Jon, a young man who lives in a marketing laboratory among teens who have been literally raised on a diet of commercials. Aside from what they see through a single window that overlooks the "real world" Rustic Village Apartment complex, with its run-down cars and regular scenes of marital discord, the teens have no contact with the real world. And they're happy for it, living in terror of an "ordinary" existence without good looks, designer clothes, and Aurabon (a drug the teens can "plug into" if they get the blues). Theirs is an Orwellian universe updated. Orwellian because it resembles *1984* but also because Saunders uses the wisdom of Orwell's "Politics in the English Language" in a rather extraordinary

Speaking of Style •

45

way. Orwell's famous essay argues that weak writing goes hand in hand with dubious political purposes. The use of the passive, pretentious diction, clichéd figurative language, verb phrases instead of simple verbs . . . For Orwell, all this isn't just bad; it's *morally* bad. Weak writing conceals meaning, which makes it an ideal language for politicians and the default language for the lazy. After all, politicians often *need* to justify the unjustifiable, and one way they can do that is through obfuscation and imprecision, by giving the impression that they're conveying information when, in fact, they're doing all they can to prevent listeners from visualizing anything untoward. As for the lazy—which we all are, at times—they don't want to bother to figure out what they mean or to work to fit words to their meaning.

Had Orwell written his critique of language in 2005 instead of 1946, we can guess that he'd have something to say about the cheerful slogans and inanities of contemporary advertising, the habitual use of marketing language in politics, business, and everyday speech. As it is, Orwell writes, "Modern writing at its worst does not consist in picking out words for the sake of their meaning and inventing images in order to make the meaning clearer. It consists in gumming together long strips of words which have already been set in order by someone else, and making the results presentable by sheer humbug."[23]

This perfectly describes Jon's language. As a result of the mind control to which he is subjected, Jon only has other people's words as he goes to express himself. The genius of Saunders's story is that it manages to use language that was designed to conceal in order to reveal. All this works because Jon isn't trying to swindle the reader as he speaks. He's *trying* to be expressive despite his impoverished language.

The opening paragraph of "Jon" consists of a long run-on sentence—a mistake—that nonetheless indicates the desire of the character to say what he means. He is doing the best he can with the language he has. And Saunders makes this work because his language *is* powerful, "wrong" as it is.

After the opening paragraph, Saunders' story continues with this:

And then nightfall would fall and our facility would fill with the sounds of quiet fast breathing from inside our Privacy Tarps as we all experimented per the techniques taught us in "It's Yours to Do With What You Like!" and what do you suspect, you had better make sure that that little gap between the main wall and the sliding wall that slides out to make your Gender Areas is like really really small. Which guess what, it wasn't.

That is all what I am saying.

Saunders is playing this for laughs, but not only for laughs, and there's an odd rightness to this mess, with its repetitions, needless words, and breathless elision of thoughts, overheard instructions, and ideas. Phrases like "nightfall would fall" or "the sliding wall that slides" are comically redundant but rhythmically satisfying. A sentence like "That is all what I am saying" mashes together two possible constructions ("That is all I am saying," "What I am saying is . . .") and in the process reveals something of Jon's passion (and dysfunction). Jon only has one mouth but wants to push both his sentences out of it at exactly the same time.

George Saunders confesses,

I didn't go to the greatest of schools as a young kid, and then I went to engineering school, and so my grammar is not the best. I'm not articulate in a conventional way, so I channel my energies into other things—dialogue, for example—where inarticulateness can actually convey passion, and, in doing so, becomes, in a perverse way, articulate. . . . [L]anguage is inherently political. So something like "like" is a sort of indicator of a larger societal dysfunction. What "like" does is allow you to join two thoughts that are grammatically distinct but associatively linked, without having to go to great lengths to make the connection. It's kind of an impressionistic device. You can say, "The truck was going so fast, like, I just went, like: Slow down, jerk?" I'm sure we stumbled across that sort of device because we needed it. It's meaningful. The same goes for euphemisms, which I love. When somebody takes great trouble not to say something, it's an incredible display. They can't say, "I'm dying." Instead they have to say, "The ongoing experience that has been my life is apparently not going to be quite as lengthy as was first suggested to me."[24]

HEMON'S EXPERIENCE in life and Saunders's experience of language are hardly universal. In fact, though I've been arguing that distinct visions result in distinct writing styles, it's clearly the case that distinct social experiences do too. I'm thinking of writers like James Kelman or Toni Cade Bambara, authors who know their community and can write from it.

And yet, perhaps the examples I've presented so far are somewhat alienating, offering up the style of writers who might be too original for some people's tastes. Neither Hemon nor Saunders is a particular devotee of the realist mode, so here's a paragraph that, on the basis of experience at least, most Americans could have written.

> *There is no God;* the revelation came to Dan Kellogg in the instant that he saw the World Trade Center South Tower fall. He lived in Cincinnati but happened to be in New York, visiting his daughter in Brooklyn Heights, with a top-floor view of Lower Manhattan, less than a mile away. He was still puzzling over the vast quantities of persistent oily smoke, and the nature of the myriad pieces of what seemed to be white cardboard fluttering within the smoke's dark column, and who and what the perpetrators and purpose of this event might have been, when, as abruptly as a girl letting fall her silken gown, the entire skyscraper dropped its sheath and vanished, with a silvery rippling noise.[25]

These are the first few sentences of John Updike's "Varieties of Religious Experience." The paragraph starts with an emphasis on explanation—this is what Dan thought, this is what he saw, this is who he was—then calmly moves into detailed observation before racing to a panicked question—*What is this all about?*—and then finishing with an erotic simile (Lord, of all things!) for the World Trade Center disaster. The style here is fluent, the observations sharp, the sensibility intelligent. Behind all this is a sense that the right detail, correctly described, will yield up meaning. Updike's prose contains existential doubt and passion while maintaining a faith in rightness, a belief in the existence of correctness and reasonableness.

HEMON, SAUNDERS, and Updike all write much more than well-made prose (or, in the case of Saunders, well-made bad prose). Back when I said well-done prose sucks, give me something more, I meant something like the work of these authors, but I have to quickly add, I don't want *you* to give me Hemon, Saunders, and Updike, because

Hemon already did Hemon, Saunders already did Saunders. The something else, the something more has to be … well, it has to be you, and here I'll segue into the how-to section of my essay, for there's a danger in my words so far, a danger that reminds me of how I used to read fashion (style!) magazines in my twenties and then house decorating magazines in my thirties. Which was not so much to improve my wardrobe or fix up my house but to assure myself of my own good taste. So: what if you suspect you may be writing well-made stories that aren't all that distinctive in terms of style? What should you *do?* The first rule always seems to be, don't try too hard. Straining after a distinctive style seems to lead one quickly into the realm of artificiality and dishonesty. Away from rather than toward a true vision. This is true on a macro and a micro level. "When a phrase is born," says Babel's narrator in "Guy de Maupassant," "it is both good and bad at the same time. The secret of its success rests in a crux that is barely discernible. One's fingertips must grasp the key, gently warming it. And then the key must be turned once, not twice."[26]

WHEN I was in college, one of my writing teachers, John Hersey, told me that no one discovers their writing voice before they're thirty. Who knows if that's true? It makes *sense,* given that "vision" seems less dependent on intelligence than experience of the world, a life lived. There being a reason why there aren't writing prodigies the way there are music prodigies. Of course, what I'm saying hardly explains Carson McCullers. Or the amount of dud writing I've encountered in Elderhostel-type writing classes. In the *Elements of Style,* E. B. White says, "Every writer, by the way he uses the language, reveals something of his spirit, his habits, his capacities, his bias. . . . No writer long remains incognito."[27] We might think of the "pulpit rhythms" of James Baldwin's writing and what we know of his life. Or the punning wry despair of Lorrie Moore.

Yet many people who want to write do remain incognito. I've read a lot of boring writing in my life but haven't met that many boring people. Not all people are writers, it's true, but many writers don't manage to spill their truest vision on the page. Perhaps E. B. White just needed to add the word *honest* to his description. If you're writing honestly, it's hard to remain incognito. Writing honestly is the challenge, though, and we're frequently incapable of it. When novelist Elizabeth Strout came to read at my college last winter, I noticed that her publishers made a lot of the fact that she'd done some stand-up comedy to help her write her novel *Amy and Isabelle.* After her reading, I asked why, thinking that she would respond by saying something about timing, or audience, or humor. But she said she wanted to know about telling the truth. "When you're a stand-up comic," she said, "you *have* to tell the truth," and you learn immediately from an audience whether you've been honest or not.

WRITERS, YOUNG and old, frequently slight themselves on the page. If I were to judge by their writing, I would have told you that my students at Colby College held only the most narrow-minded, racist attitudes about the war in Iraq. During their preclass hubbub, they never once broached the matter. Finally, fearing they were the apathetic lunks that the young are so often made out to be, I asked them what they thought about the war. Their response was complex and conflicted. In the end, they didn't know what to do with their desire to believe what they were told, given their across-the-board suspicion about what they heard. But none of this translated into their work, which, in the rare cases when they broached the matter, had all the depth of a Popeye cartoon. Another example: I have a good friend who is an edgy, obsessive, politically correct woman who strikes me, most of the time, as perfectly well behaved, sensitive, and furious. To read her (well-made) prose, you'd think she was a nice, observant person. And that's all. You'd never guess how angry she is. For all these writers, there's a translation problem; too much is being edited out, and what's largely getting edited out is contradiction. But confusion itself might lead us (collectively) to a more nuanced style. Look at Robert Stone, with his characters who feel something, then unfeel it, then question their unfeeling. But there's nothing confused about Stone's perception of the confusion. It's there. He acknowledges it. His prose about confusion isn't confused. And what's most important, Stone doesn't retreat into tentativeness (that "Well, maybe this isn't right?" voice that holds so many writers back), and he doesn't hesitate to own his perceptions when they aren't (especially when they aren't) neat or easy to articulate.

HOW TO get there, though? How to figure out what your vision is so you can effectively translate it onto the page? I'm finally ready to offer up my words of wisdom.

First, be yourself.

Second, be someone else.

TO EXPLAIN: One shouldn't feel obliged in fiction. You don't "have" to write like anybody save yourself. If you can access that self—if you can translate that self onto the page—you've done what you need to do. George Saunders says,

> What took me a really long time was realizing that just using my internal voice was all right, and it was the one I actually had to use. That internal voice was not anti-artistic, exactly, but it wasn't one I'd seen or heard. I can remember thinking, You mean I should write that way, just like I think? It was really liberating for me to say, "I'm going to be a goofball for the rest of my life. I'm going to be a ninety-year-old guy with a fart cushion." It took a great weight off my shoulders.
>
> There's a whole list of things I can't do in fiction writing, that I wouldn't even try—no, I have tried them, and that's why I know I can't do them. I only started having fun when I started saying, "Okay, I can't write a straight sentence. I can't describe nature. I don't really care what happens when a divorcing couple sits down in a café. I just don't care." When I turned away from those things and turned toward things I like to do— dialogue, humor—then suddenly everything opened up for me. But I'm always aware of writing around things I can't do, and I've come to think that that's actually what "style" is—an avoidance of your deficiencies.[28]

Saunders had to work to figure out what it was he couldn't do, but he seems to have had a fair amount of clarity about his internal voice. Others feel fuzzier about their brains. You know—on the one hand, you know what you think; on the other hand, there's what you think about what you think and then what you think about *that* . . . and then which is what you really think? Figure it all out, and you'll be on your way.

A LOT of writers and writing books suggest that you discover your own style by paying attention to the prose style of other writers, even by copying it. John Hersey used to say that one shouldn't worry about copying another writer's style because your copy won't be like the other writer's. It will be like you *and* the other writer. In the discrepancy between your imitation and the real thing, you may find your own voice.

For instance, consider the following two paragraphs, written by one of the five authors (Carver, Cheever, Hemon, Saunders, and Updike) whom I've discussed in this essay.

> The few passengers in the cars looked out through the glass and thought it strange to find these people on the platform, making ready to board a train at this time of night. What business could have taken them out? This was the hour when people should be thinking of going to bed. The kitchens in the houses up on the hills behind the station were clean and orderly; the dishwashers had long ago finished their cycle, all things were in their places. Night-lights burned in children's bedrooms. A few teenaged girls might still be reading novels, their fingers twisting a strand of hair as they did so. But television sets were going off now. Husbands and wives were making their own preparations for the night. The half-dozen or so passengers, sitting by themselves in the two cars, looked through the glass and wondered about the three people on the platform.
>
> They saw a heavily made-up, middle-aged woman wearing a rose-colored knit dress mount the steps and enter the train. Behind her came a younger woman dressed in a summer blouse and skirt who clutched a handbag. They were followed onto the train by an old man who moved slowly and who carried himself in a dignified manner. The old man had white hair and a white silk cravat, but he was without shoes. The passengers naturally assumed that the three people boarding were together; and they felt sure that whatever these people's business had been that night, it had not come to a happy conclusion.[29]

THIS SOUNDS . . . well, this sounds a lot like Cheever, but, in fact, the paragraphs are from Carver's short story "Train." Actually "Train" doesn't make much sense till you realize what it is—a continuation of John Cheever's short story "Five Forty Eight." "Train" picks up where the Cheever story ends, at a train station where a woman has just pulled a gun on her former boss/lover and made him grovel in the dirt before she agrees to spare his life. Cheever's story is told from the point of view of the comically insensitive boss, trying to avoid his former secretary as he rides the 5:48 train home from Manhattan. Carver's story is told largely from the secretary's point of view, just after she's crossed the tracks to catch a train back into Manhattan.

In the paragraphs I've quoted, Carver's positively garrulous compared to his earlier self, using adjectives and adverbs, writing longer complex sentences, dreamily speculating about other lives, and even slipping into an omniscient voice that has a loving edge and admits of a curiosity that extends beyond the immediate.

And yet you could argue that this imitation of Cheever's style, whether conscious or not (certainly the inspiration for the story was conscious), reveals a lot about Carver's style. As rich as this paragraph is, it's not nearly as rich as Cheever. In all the places these paragraphs don't quite sound like Cheever (in the lack of lengthy description, the relative uniformity of sentence length, and the avoidance of multiple modifiers), you see Carveresque restraint peeking through.

MY HUSBAND is a painter, and one of the ways I figure out what I think is by rehearsing ideas with him. As I was trying to explain the thesis of this essay, I said, "Like, well, you know how there are a thousand Maine landscapes, but a Marsden Hartley is a Marsden Hartley?" He nodded his head. Sure, he knew. He was the one who introduced me to Hartley in the first place. But then he reminded me that a lot of Hartley's early work was derivative, that Hartley only *came* to his vision by working through the vision of others. Visual artists don't develop a distinct style till they figure out how to work in their medium, and they do that, in part, by copying.

What's more, vision develops through the arc of a life. More reminders from my husband: it's not an ascending ladder. Things plateau. In moments of intense focus, there are discoveries. Then you fall back. When you're painting, you're painfully aware of the derivative nature of the work, of imitation, and then at a certain point, you realize you're not imitating anyone anymore.

Unfortunately, once you finally find your way to your own voice, to a distinctive style, you run the risk of imitating yourself. Philip Guston seemed revolutionary when he embraced (what some people called) abstract impressionism but even more revolutionary when he broke away from it, at the height of his career, to do his cartoony KKK figures. Though he was lambasted for the move at the time, it now seems like a decision of artistic genius.

Since we all use language and most of us write, whether we're writers or not, the parallel with the visual arts might seem irrelevant, but the language of fiction isn't everyday language. In our apprenticeship (and regretfully my personal experience confirms that an apprenticeship can be lifelong), we *are* testing our materials. We're seeing what we can do, then making the huge leap from what we *want* to do to what we *can* do. Then, if we stay with it long enough, if we're lucky in our talents, we'll be able to translate our inner voice onto the page. And *that* will be our style. And it won't be well done, for who ever heard of a well-done inner voice?

Cry, Cry, Cry
HANDLING EMOTION IN FICTION

Last october, I gave birth to my first child. In the months before my son was born, my writer friends—my *female* writer friends— uncheerily warned me about what motherhood would mean for my literary future, telling me first, of course, that I'd never find time to write. And that I'd never find time to read, unless I didn't mind, say, propping a book on my son's head while I nursed him, and even then I could count on being too overwhelmed for that particular gymnastic feat. But actually I've read lots in the past ten months. Books and books. In fact, by my bedside is a title I've read numerous times. It's called *Baby Faces*. Not all that well known, so let me summarize . . . well, no, I'll just quote a bit. Each page features a photograph of a baby, underneath which is a single word describing the baby's expression: "Happy." "Sad." "Puzzled." "Worried." You get the idea. And then it closes, "Dirty." "Clean." "Tired." "Fast asleep." My son likes this book. He likes it a lot. We read it, and we laugh uproariously at each page. "Happy." We laugh. "Sad." That's a riot. We laugh. "Worried." That doesn't concern us. We laugh. Art, according to Leo Tolstoy, is the means of transferring emotion from one man's heart to another. And as much as my son and I like this book, emotion, I have to confess, is not being transferred from one man's heart to another. Or one baby's, although I do get peculiarly choked up every time I consider that beautiful "fast asleep" conclusion. But that's another matter. Suffice it to say that conveying emotion is not merely a matter of depicting emotion. A picture of emotion won't get you, as a writer, where you want to go. In fact, it might get you where you don't want to go: with people laughing at tears.

TRUE, THE author of *Baby Faces* is not aiming for art. But we are. So back to Tolstoy and his essay "What Is Art?" "The activity of art," Tolstoy writes, "is based on the fact that a man, receiving through his sense of hearing or sight another man's expression of feeling, is capable of experiencing the emotion which moved the man who expressed it."[1] Literature, then, is a form of communion. Of course, not everyone holds this to be so. "It is a bad time out in the world for emotion," Maria tells a prisoner in Rainer Werner Fassbinder's *The Marriage of Maria Braun.* And why, asks Edna O'Brien, is this so? Why is feeling—at least feeling in contemporary literature—in hiding? It might be the influence of the chic, O'Brien concludes, or some mix of the chic with the serious, or the deadening nonsense of pop songs, but mostly it is the "prevailing ethos of literary criticism" which makes fun of true feeling.[2] Is this as true in the States as it is, to O'Brien's mind, in Britain? Here, I think, true feeling's greatest enemy is kitsch, which makes us feel but obscures the object of our feeling, so in the end, all we're doing is having a lovefest with ourselves, with our capacity to emote. True feeling survives nonetheless. It is there in the books O'Brien most loves. It is there in her own work, so O'Brien can conclude her essay "It's a Bad Time Out There for Emotion" by writing, "Books are the Grail for what is deepest, more mysterious and least expressible within ourselves. They are our soul's skeleton. If we were to forget that, it would prefigure how false and feelingless we could become."[3]

My thoughts here presuppose O'Brien's value system. And Tolstoy's. Which is to say that whatever else you look for in fiction, you also read to be moved, truly and honestly moved. So given this, how are we to do what Tolstoy asks us? How are we to do this given that a mere depiction of emotion isn't enough to convey emotion?

The title of my essay—"Cry, Cry, Cry"—is actually stolen from a CD by Dar Williams, Lucy Kaplansky, and Richard Shindell. The CD *Cry, Cry, Cry* consists, for the most part, of covers of songs by folk artists who started touring in the eighties or nineties. Williams, Kaplansky, and Shindell doing the work of artists they love. The title suits me, both because of my subject—handling emotion in fiction— and my method—I'm going to present my version of other people's ideas. In six tracks.

TRACK 1. *William Kittredge, "If you're not risking sentimentality, you're not close to your inner self."[4]*

Sentimentality is bad. Writers should *risk* sentimentality, not *achieve* sentimentality. So what, exactly, is sentimentality? I asked my husband, hoping he'd give me the conventional take on the matter. "Well, it's saccharin," he said. "Like a Hallmark card." Writers should risk becoming a Hallmark card? I don't think so. What we don't like about Hallmark cards—and my husband stumbled into this next—is that they seem insincere. And that's not what Kittredge wants us to risk. He wants us to risk too much emotion, possibly to overdo the real stuff, simply because we are willing to address it in the first place. Presumably Kittredge is defining sentimentality as an excess of sentiment, not as inauthentic emotion—and the challenge is to feel fully. "Dare you see a soul *at the White Heat*?" Emily Dickinson asks.[5] And the truth is: we don't, not always.

An example from TV commercials: During my pregnancy, I regularly saw an ad in which a handsome older man, with plenty of hair on his head, tells about a lovely day with his grandchildren. As I remember it, the man narrates this memory from the well-manicured lawn of his attractive Victorian home. And then the camera captures his words by panning over several generations of his family yukking it up on the front porch. But the man is telling a sad story—or so his tone implies—he is telling about a lovely day when he was nonetheless too tired to go upstairs and get his camera to take a picture of his grandkids. The man emphasizes the pain of this. He was—it's true!—too tired to get his camera. And then we learn that this ad is for a drug that relieves some of the symptoms of chemotherapy.

This ad enraged me. And yet, as infrequently as I watch TV, there it was, an irritating refrain to my pregnancy. What angered me must be fairly obvious: Grandpa could have asked one of the kids to scuttle up the stairs for the camera. Grandpa had a lot more than a little exhaustion to worry about if he was having serious rounds of chemo. But presumably an advertisement geared to making us feel good about an item—the drug company's product—doesn't want us picturing bald heads, mouth sores, vomiting, and worse. This is sort of like the passive voice inflated to an ad campaign. What's most important is that the viewer fails to get a clear picture of what the symptoms of chemotherapy can be like.

Around the time of this ad, the American Diabetes Association produced a commercial that most markets refused to run. In it, a man removes his foot—a prosthetic foot, it turns out—from his boot. A voice-over says, "Give diabetes an inch, and it'll take a foot." Shocking, yes. But true enough. And apparently the American public didn't want to consider it. Not, at least, in the hours when they were trying to relax in front of the TV.

Kittredge's challenge—the go-there, say-that, make-yourself-squirm school of advice—assumes an aesthetics of cost. It touches on the whole line of thinking that we resist our inner selves, and yet what is most uncomfortable to explore may have the most value. It is hard to reject such a notion. If our best material isn't in our inner selves, where is it? On the surface, where we're all wearing (as Leonard Woolf would have it) some form of mask? Even so, I can't help thinking of an old Bill Cosby routine, which I present here as half fiction since I may be misremembering it. Cosby, in his doofus dad role, asks what something—smoking pot, I'm guessing—feels like, and he's told that it makes you feel like yourself, only more intensely so, and Cosby deadpans, "But what if you're an asshole?" For fiction writers, the answer probably is, "If you are, you are. Put it out there anyway." Our passions and our griefs are what we have to offer.

Emily Dickinson:
Take all away from me, but leave me Ecstasy
And I am richer then than all my Fellow men—[6]

TRACK 2. *Raymond Carver, "A good book is an honest one."*[7]

Fiction, we know, is not true. It is a lie. And yet we insist on honesty in fiction. We want fidelity to the real world so we can lose ourselves in the imagined one. The nature of that fidelity varies, according to the aesthetic of the writer. Steven Millhauser has a man marry a frog in one of his stories. We would not accept such antics from Chekhov. Artists need to be true to their intentions. But whatever their intentions are, they also need to be emotionally honest. In part, this simply means that they need to depict their characters' emotional lives accurately. Without an explanation of some sort, we won't, for instance, accept a character's joy at the untimely death of a child. As a writer, you must have a sense of how people are and then depict it.

You must feel truly and then find an appropriate container for your emotions. This doesn't sound so complicated, but it turns out there are lots of ways to be emotionally dishonest as a writer, to slight what you know to be true about people, because you're trying so hard to write a good story. Sentimentality and coldness are falsehoods, two extremes of dishonesty. Sentimentality gives a moment more than it has earned, coldness less. But there's plenty of middle ground as well. When it comes to emotion, you can be imprecise, inauthentic, and manipulative . . . all without really trying. Writing is difficult, and a little dishonesty makes it easier. Say not quite what you mean, or genuinely believe to be true, and you'll be able to finish your paragraph. Get your exact thought down, and you may have to wait and wait, for your brain to make a connection; for your imagination to come up with the right word, image, or idea. Your inexact thought won't produce as good a book, but it will come faster. Reason #322 that writing sucks.

TRACK 3. *James Baldwin, "Sentimentality, the ostentatious parading of excessive and spurious emotion, is the mark of dishonesty, the inability to feel."*[8]

The sentimental didn't always have such a bad reputation. The word itself is obviously an outgrowth of the word *sentiment,* which was in the English language by the fourteenth century and meant, originally, "a sensation," "a physical feeling," and then an "opinion or view as to what is right or agreeable."

The words *sentimental* and *sentimentality* appeared in the middle to late eighteenth century. Neither word had a negative connotation until the late nineteenth century, when the word *sentimentalism* came to mean the "disposition to attribute undue importance to sentimental considerations, or to be governed by sentiment in opposition to reason." Around the same time, *sentimentality* appears as an "affectation of sensibility." And the word gets an increasingly negative sense as time goes on, till *sentimentality* suggests not just inauthenticity but hypocrisy.[9]

The Victorians are notorious sentimentalists. Ask people to name a work of sentimental literature, and invariably they mention Tennyson's "In Memoriam," with its excess of grief, or Charles Dickens's death of Little Nell in *The Old Curiosity Shop:*

Her couch was dressed with here and there some winter berries and green leaves, gathered in a spot she had been used to favor. "When I die, put near me something that has loved the light, and had the sky above it always." Those were her words. She was dead. Dear, gentle, patient, noble Nell was dead.[10]

According to Fred Kaplan, author of *Sacred Tears: Sentimentality in Victorian Literature,* we moderns read Victorian sentimentality inappropriately, failing to see it in the context in which it was produced. The Victorians' intellectual inheritance was the eighteenth century, the age of rationalism and Hobbesian pessimism but also the age of philosophical idealism with its optimistic view of human nature, as propounded by David Hume, Adam Smith, and the like. The Victorians' own era, the nineteenth century, was the age of Hegel and his discovery of universal reason. It was the age of utilitarianism, rationalism, and scientific determinism. But it was also an age of faith in the "moral sentiments." Which is to say, the belief that people would act correctly, morally, because of innate feelings. Like Dickens, many Victorians held that people were innately good; evil was a product of unfortunate social conditioning. "Sentimentality in the Western tradition," writes Kaplan, "takes its force from a keen awareness of the mixed nature of human nature. It is an attempt, among other things, to generate or at least strengthen the possibility of the triumph of the feelings and the heart over self-serving calculation."[11] We may scoff at the death of Little Nell in Charles Dickens's *The Old Curiosity Shop,* but, in Kaplan's reading of it, the scene seems positively noble. But as Kaplan admits, "As we move further away from Eden into history, the moral ideal becomes less a part of our daily lives and inappropriate to depictions, especially in the novel, of the truths of daily existence."[12]

Certainly, by the middle of the twentieth century, sentimentality in serious literature was a firm no-no. In the 1938 anthology *Readings for Creative Writers,* George Williams writes that sentimentality is "goodness and pure emotion, without intellect" and that sentimentality puts "a preposterous value on everything."[13]

WHEN I was living in Cambridge and teaching fiction at Tufts University, I had an experience that is fairly common, I think, for people who teach creative writing. For a workshop class, a student—I'll call her Beth—submitted a story about a lovely girl, a "saint," who was hanging out at the lake with her family. Everyone looks at this girl as she canoes about the lake and then docks to wander along shore, because there is something so fabulous about her—she exudes a sort of honesty and carefree manner, a love of life, an enthusiastic buoyancy, etc., etc. When she sees a crying child, she stops to reaffix a Band-Aid on his knee. She gamely returns tennis balls that flirting boys lob in her direction. In the evening, she and her family return to their rustic cabin, barbecue some juicy burgers, and discuss summers past. The next day, the family drives home. On the way, a truck comes across the median on the turnpike and wrecks the car, killing the girl and leaving the rest of the family with broken bones. At the funeral, everyone weeps and weeps. Someone plays a tape of the song "Forever Young." The girl, the story concludes, was a saint after all.

When my class discussed this story, they said all the things you might imagine about the need to develop a more complex character, the importance of avoiding clichés, the danger of a sentimental conclusion. There wasn't—one student noted—a true story here, because the character was simply the victim of circumstances. But, Beth protested—despite the class ban on speaking in workshop—her brother had just died this way.

"Oh, my God," I offered and wrapped things up.

After class, Beth and I met to talk about the story, though, of course, I didn't quite feel like that was what we should do. I said how sorry I was to hear about her brother. She said it was her half-brother actually, a boy she'd never lived with but was close to all the same, and he had died a few months earlier. I told her that my sister had died young, and I continued to try to say what I could. As I did, Beth started to cry, though she was struggling not to, and I wondered how much I should encourage her to talk about things or whether I was intruding. (Knowing that I had wanted all the comfort in the world after my sister's death has not provided me with a guide to how I should treat others in similar circumstances.) As I sat with her, in those silly little chairs that they had at the university—the ones with the little beige islands that come around your front—she apologized for crying. "It's OK," I said. She started to wipe the tears away from her face with the pad of her forefinger, and each time she did this, she tucked her finger into her fist, as if she had to put each tear someplace. Then she said—haltingly—"It's just . . . it's affecting everything." And then in a very small voice, "You know?" Now the thing is, of course, I did—I do—know, not that I was able to convey that very well. I told her how brave she was to write about something so close to her. And some time later, we parted.

Excessive and spurious emotion was not Beth's problem. She felt her loss, and she felt it honestly and appropriately. And she was capable of expressing her emotion clearly and directly, as she did with her broken sentence to me. You could not say she was putting a preposterous value on everything. And yet her story was hopelessly sentimental. How come? Knowing the definition of sentimentality won't necessarily help you avoid it if you don't also recognize the *forms* sentimentality takes in literature. Oscar Wilde once said that sentimentality is when you're expected to love a character more than God would. It makes easy (and foolish) use of the ideal. Clearly Beth had done just that. But, to her credit, she hadn't done any worse than Charles Dickens.

ACCORDING TO George Williams, another form of sentimentality is unrestrained expression of emotion.[14] Here is a paragraph from a student of David Huddle's as reproduced in Huddle's essay "On Restraint." In it, an angry daughter, Lizzie, confronts her mother, Marilyn, in rather dramatic fashion:

> Lizzie pulled the trigger and exploded her skull into the room. Marilyn recoiled as Lizzie's juices splattered on her dress and dribbled down the beige walls. Blood gurgled in pulsing waves from Lizzie's shredded, gaping head. The body lay still in its horror—except for the final convulsions of Lizzie's free fingers—tap, tap, tap—on the floor. And then the dead silence. Winston's plaid beret had been disturbed from its position on the brass coat-rack; it lay meekly on the floor—approached by the widening red pool.[15]

Oh, my, where to start? I can hear myself with this student: "Uh . . . you could cut some of the adjectives." The dishonesty here is thorough. This is a suicide, but a suicide that owes nothing to what the emotions of a suicidal daughter and her grief-stricken mother are like or even what the physics of a gory death are.

Compare this to Stewart O'Nan's story, "Please Help Find." The setup is essentially the same—miserable daughter, dumbfounded mother. Only every choice—about point of view, structure, content, language, detail, scene—that O'Nan makes differs from every choice Huddle's student made. Most importantly, perhaps, the moment of greatest drama—the successful suicide—is off the page, done as a flash-forward in the story's final line. The moment of second greatest drama—the unsuccessful suicide—is done as a memory and placed a page away from the story's opening. We know it is important, of course, but we're not overwhelmed by it right away. Instead, what's forefronted, in the body of the story, is a period of relative happiness: the daughter Janice's first day of college, the drive upstate to the campus, and the hours in which Janice supposes she might just be all right after all. The happiness is truly relative, for Janice is, for most of the story, irritable. She's annoyed at her mother, disappointed in her destination. Just when she would most like her mother to depart, she needs to suffer through the inconvenience of Lonnie the dog's disappearance and the subsequent search. Still, it is when Janice is merely irritable (as opposed to suicidal) that we're able to get a sense of who she is and what some of her issues are. We see her, too, as she experiences a small reversal, the desperate desire for her mother to be OK. And we see her, most importantly, when she experiences a bit of true pleasure. She concedes that she likes her roommate. She feels passing affection for Lonnie and even the urge to hug her mother. On a second read, we might acknowledge that suicide is all over this story. It's there from the first line—"Why was it, Janice thought, that everything took longer than you wanted? Like life."[16] There are other clues as well. The sentence: "The Mellaril seemed to be working or that's what her mother thought."[17] But on a first read of "Please Help Find," the suicide steps back a little. It gives life a chance. And even on a second, third, and fourth read, life asserts itself so honestly and truly—everything about this story and these characters seems so believable—that the story's final line makes me cry every time, even when I know it is coming.

> The bell tower was lit, and as she paused a minute, breathing in the cool air, the bells chimed a high, light ringing like Sunday, like the cities in Europe she always wanted to visit, and Janice thought of her mother and what had happened today, how it was a mystery, how it had changed everything between

them, and that was the feeling she would remember just a few months later, before her last, successful attempt: how badly she'd wanted to be happy here, and how it had seemed, for one still and perfect moment, almost possible.[18]

Sometimes, not always, it is wise to avoid the actual moment of greatest trauma—or passion—in fiction, because characters may be more generic at the exact instance they learn of a death, or have an orgasm, or win the lottery than they are just before or after such moments. There are infinite ways to express pain or pleasure or surprise, but there may be only so many ways to say, "Oh, my God, no," or "Oh, my God, yes," or "Yippee." What the structure of O'Nan's story wisely recognizes is that there is something far more painful than a generic suicide, and that is the suicide of a very particular person who has tried (even if halfheartedly) to live. "Please Help Find" acknowledges, too, that avoiding sentimentality isn't so much a matter of restraining emotion as of being precise about emotion, since the "control" that O'Nan exercises is not a matter of repressing the truth but recognizing and telling a complex truth. This involves, of course, an ability to articulate contradictions—for example, the concomitant hollowness, sense of power, and satisfaction Janice feels during her unsuccessful suicide attempt.

ONE WAY to repress the truth is to avoid it, to transfer emotion from the thing itself to a symbol of the thing. George Williams cites, by way of example, a mother crying over her dead infant's little booties.[19] But any time a symbol seems clunky in fiction, this form of sentimentality may be the culprit. Flowers falling lifelessly to a grave. The disenchanted wife's wedding ring sitting in her jewelry box. The perfume bottle that recalls the smells of the old woman's youth. We shrink from these symbols because they're clichés but also because they're routinely employed to carry emotions that (presumably) the story itself does not carry. Better to let a symbol work as names do in Toni Cade Bambara's "Gorilla, My Love." In the story, adult lies incense a little girl named Mabel. Her anger focuses on grown-ups trying to play "trick up" with words and names. Mabel's particularly mad about her uncle's attempt to wheedle out of an earlier promise to marry her. The uncle tells her that his promise doesn't mean anything because he was Hunca Bubba when he made the promise—Hunca Bubba is Mabel's nickname for her uncle—and now he's Jefferson Winston Hall.

In all things, Mabel prefers to call it as she sees it. Which is why, to her mind, "Havmore" potato chips are so fine. You do indeed want to have more Havmore potato chips. And which is why the title of the religious movie, *Gorilla, My Love,* so irks. As she says, "When you fixed to watch a gorilla picture you don't wanna get messed around with Sunday School stuff."[20] Words have meanings—Mabel has figured this out—and pretending that something doesn't mean what it says it means is one form of adult duplicity. Something that Mabel won't stand for. But, of course, as a child, she doesn't always have a choice in the matter, an injustice that makes her so mad that, at the story's close, unable to find the word she wants, she says what she doesn't quite mean and then bursts into tears. Her sorrow may not move us the way Janice's despair affects us in O'Nan's story, but we trust the honesty of the emotion all the same. As adults, we cannot be upset that Mabel does not get to marry her uncle, but we still feel her disappointment and anger with adults and their lies. But these emotions aren't our only ones as we read, for this isn't, despite Mabel's closing tears, a sad story. As readers, we can feel with a character or not; emotion is transferred, all the same, as long as we feel with a piece's narrative impulse. Here, the narrative impulse has to do with a certain pleasure we take in seeing the little guy, or girl, in this case, resist the powers that be.

THAT MABEL arrives at a final moment of frustration with adults doesn't surprise us as readers. It seems a natural place to leave her, even though we can imagine a happier (to her mind) ending for "Gorilla, My Love." It would be foolish to take Mabel to that happier ending, of course, since such a happy ending would be inappropriate, in a practical and a moral sense. Little girls don't marry their adult uncles, thank you. And it would be foolish for aesthetic reasons as well, for one final form of sentimentality is the forced conclusion, a brand of sentimentality that comes (according to George Williams) from "faith in the quick conversion."[21] In our own time, such faith, such belief in neat redemption, is at the source of much popular art and literature. The hooker rescued from her profession in the movie

Pretty Woman, for example. But, says fiction writer Steve Stern, if you're a serious writer, "You're responsible for following the emotions that are a consequence of your story's conflict rather than imposing a solution that is a neat contrivance. Imposing your will on a story and character who could not possibly arrive at a certain place results in a dishonest ending."[22]

In William Trevor's *Reading Turgenev,* Mary Louise Dallon marries a man many years her senior, because she doesn't think anyone else will have her and she wants to get off her family's farm and into town. From the wedding night on, everything goes wrong. The marriage is never consummated. The couple never truly communicate. Eventually, Mary Louise finds the love she needs in the affection of an ill cousin; her husband, Elmer, finds it in the bottle. On the night that Mary Louise and her cousin finally, however timidly, confess their love for one another, the cousin dies. Mary Louise breaks down when she receives this shocking news, retreating even further from Elmer, only taking what pleasure she can in the love she had for her cousin, the love he had for her. In the end, Mary Louise doesn't get to have a happy marriage. She doesn't even get to have a troubled, unhappy affair. She gets to be institutionalized—for thirty-one years—as a crazy woman and then to have what might seem like a rather slight reward for a life of pain. She is, to the clergyman whose thoughts close the novella, "prosperous," because "passion came, like consummation in the end. For thirty-one years she'd clung to a refuge in which her love affair could spread itself, a safe house offering sanctuary. For thirty-one years she passed as mad and was at peace."[23] In other words, the happy ending here is that Mary Louise, at least for her thirty-one years in a psychiatric institution, was able to daydream about her cousin. And then she is taken from the institution, returned to the community, because as Elmer—himself a ruin of a man—explains, "Nowadays it's what's being done."[24]

Honesty of emotion in literature is a burden—a "terrible responsibility" in Steve Stern's words, because it "can mean following characters to the source of their pain."[25] That is, of course, where William Trevor goes, and once he goes there he can't impose neat redemption on Mary Louise's or Elmer's lives. He can't have recourse to a sentimental close.

But enough with sentimentality. Enough with what we shouldn't do. What should we do?

TRACK 4. *T. S. Eliot, "The only way of expressing emotion in the form of art is by finding an 'objective correlative'; in other words, a set of objects, a situation, a chain of events which shall be the formula of that particular emotion; such that when the external facts, which must terminate in sensory experience, are given, the emotion is immediately invoked."*[26]

Emotion is an interior feeling, but in fiction we reveal it through the exterior. I quoted Tolstoy at the start of this essay, but I cut short his definition of art. Here's some of what I left out:

> Art is a human activity, consisting in this, that one man consciously, by means of external signs, hands on to others feelings he has lived through, and that other people are infected by these feelings, and also experience them.[27]

The phrase I want to emphasize here is "by means of external signs." And here it is again, the same boring advice you've probably been hearing throughout your writing career: show, don't tell; show, don't tell; show, don't tell. But show what?

Well, emotion, of course, but this doesn't simply mean our characters should be constantly grimacing and smirking so we know what they're feeling, though physical gestures and facial expressions—not to mention dialogue—are some of the things we can use to convey emotion.

HERE'S DAN Chaon in the story "The Illustrated Encyclopedia of the Animal Kingdom," conveying two characters' mutual discomfort at a sperm bank:

> She gave him a kind of test-tube with a screw-on lid and cleared her throat, shifting her weight in those chunky white shoes, and she opened a door and said that there were some magazines he could look at if he wished. She might have used the word "peruse."
> He glanced in and there were some old *Playboy* and *Penthouse* magazines on the table next to the toilet. He nodded, not meeting her eyes. What was there to say?[28]

No need to use the word *embarrassment* here. The gestures convey everything, as they do later in the story when Chaon is trying to convey his male protagonist's complicated loneliness, his tender distress, later in life and at a particularly disconnected moment in his life, about the child he once—perhaps? who knows?—had.

That said, "make it physical" and "use external signs" are two different pieces of advice. The former can get you the kind of prose that many of my undergraduates write. Lots of tingly flesh and butterflies in the stomach and tears coursing down cheeks, and still no emotion being conveyed. And this is because in the end, you don't want to present emotion in fiction, you want to present what gives rise to an emotion. The disappointing fair in James Joyce's "Araby," the litany of motherly advice in Jamaica Kincaid's one-sentence short story, "Girl," the death of a child in Raymond Carver's "A Small, Good Thing." And once you present what gives rise to an emotion, you don't need to depict emotion—you don't then need to tell your reader how to feel, for your reader will already know how to feel.

An example: In the opening pages of Oscar Hijuelos's *The Mambo Kings Sing Songs of Love,* Eugenio tries to get his uncle, Cesar, to wake up from a drunken stupor to watch an old *I Love Lucy* episode in which the uncle and Nestor, Eugenio's father, long dead, appear as musical guests from Cuba. On screen, Nestor and Cesar are a triumph. Off screen, Cesar can barely be roused. How does Eugenio feel about the TV show, about this "item of eternity," as he calls it? Well, we don't need to know. We can guess. We can guess because we get so much good material in the novel's opening pages. We witness how eager Eugenio is to see the show and to make sure Cesar joins him. We learn what Eugenio remembered about his father the first time he saw the *Lucy* rerun. We see exactly how his father and uncle look on TV. The opening chapter closes with this paragraph about the rerun's final moments, after the brothers have left the stage:

> The show continued on its course. A few gags followed: A costumed bull with flowers wrapped around its horns came out dancing an Irish jig, its horns poking into Ricky's bottom and so exasperating him that his eyes bugged out, he slapped his forehead and started speaking a thousand-words-a-second Spanish. But at that point it made no difference to me, the miracle had passed, the resurrection of a man, Our Lord's prom-

ise which I then believed, with its release from pain, release from the troubles of this world.[29]

We must show the exterior world in order to render the interior world. As counterintuitive, says novelist Rick Russo, as this might seem, "the more we're expected to understand the interior, the more vivid the exterior has to be."[30]

But this doesn't mean interior thoughts can't be presented, as this final paragraph from Hijuelos makes clear. Still, the character's thoughts must arise in a meaningful way from what has come before. An objective correlative is correlative precisely because there is a correspondence between the external material and the emotion that is being conveyed. As Janet Burroway notes in *Writing Fiction,* "In Eliot's insight, the objects, situation, and events of a particular work contain its particular effect, and if they do *not* contain the desired emotional effect, that effect cannot be produced in that work, either by its statement in abstractions or by appeal to outside symbols."[31]

Steve Stern is saying the same thing when he advises against naming emotions because "the label itself dissolves the feeling. You trap emotion by assigning it an adjective or a metaphor, but if you give gesture and response then you have an image that frees the reader to react."[32] Had Hijuelos's Eugenio told us it was both wonderful and disturbing to see his dead father on TV, that it was heartbreaking to see his uncle in his heyday when he was now a ruin of a man, we'd have felt, ironically, nothing. We'd have wanted, ironically again, for Hijuelos to stand back a little from his emotions so he could present them.

TRACK 5. *Anton Chekhov, "When you . . . wish to move your reader to pity, try to be colder. It will give a kind of backdrop to . . . grief, make it stand out more. . . . Yes, be cold."*[33]

When my student Beth—the one who had written the sentimental story about a sibling's death—handed in her second story for class, I was shocked. Because it was a good story, and I'd already made up my mind about her. She was sensitive. She was intelligent. But she couldn't write. She'd struggled with the revision of her original story, and I'd ended up telling her what I'd thought from the start: she was too close to the material to write about it effectively. I quoted Virginia

Woolf—"There must be great freedom from reality"—and talked about how hard it is to let your imagination work freely (and for the good of a story) when you're familiar with the truth of a matter. I said, in other words, the standard things that creative writing teachers say in such situations. I might have quoted Chekhov as well. "Yes, be cold." Of course, Chekhov, who we commonly think of as a master of human emotion, is not advocating cold work—not the superduper irony of our own era or the emotional blankness of, say, a Robbe-Grillet. Chekhov is advocating coldness as method.

But what exactly is behind such advice, especially given the quote I started with—the one about risking sentimentality? Why should you be cold? Of what use is emotional distance? I'm circling around a point I've already made. The way to get to emotion is to present what gives rise to the emotion, not to give the emotion itself. A story or a movie that opens with someone crying is not moving. How could it be? We don't know what the tears are about. We don't know anything about the person who is crying. All we have is the emotion, and that, by itself, is not moving. To be moved we need to have a true encounter with something, the sort of encounter that coldness and emotional distance can provide.

Creating emotional distance isn't "merely" a psychological issue, a matter of deciding when you're ready to write something. It is a craft issue that relates to everything from what part of a story you're going to tell (as Stewart O'Nan's story proves) to who is going to tell it. Why is Rufus a better protagonist for James Agee's *A Death in the Family* than his mother? Partially because—as a boy—he's not yet 100 percent connected to his emotions, so he is capable, for instance, of bragging about his father's death to win the approval of his schoolmates. (And isn't that a heartbreaking scene?)

IN READING *Turgenev,* the death of Robert, Mary Louise Dallon's cousin, is a shock, and an unbearably painful one for Mary Louise. Trevor times the death only hours after Mary Louise tells Robert about her troubled marriage, on the day when Robert first kisses Mary Louise. That night, we are told, Robert has a dream. We are given the contents of the dream, then told how—in the dream— Robert "put his arm around his cousin's waist and as they walked on the strand they talked about his father. In that moment Robert died."[34] The chapter ends with this line. No further comment. Two chapters later, when we return to the death, it is with little emotion. It is the morning after the death. Robert's uncle receives a man with a message, but the actual message is left off the page. Later, Robert's aunt goes to visit her sister, Robert's mother, and we learn that "They sat together in the kitchen for most of the day. Mrs. Dallon making tea and toast in the afternoon, and poaching an egg for each of them." We learn what they talk about—"the time when they were girls together, before their marriages; about when the men they'd married first came into their lives, and the different lives they'd had because of that."[35] There is a coldness in the method here, a dry-eyed listing of fact. This happened, then this, then this. At the end of the day, Robert's mother insists that Mrs. Dallon take some grapes home with her—a request that, in the context of her loss, seems particularly painful. Only Trevor never says that.

Later, we see the moment when Mary Louise learns of Robert's death. From Mrs. Dallon's perspective. Since she doesn't know about the cousins' adult relationship, her emotional distance from her daughter's loss makes her peculiarly well equipped to narrate the moment when Mary Louise registers that loss: "Mrs. Dallon considered it odd of her younger daughter to faint when she was told of her cousin's death since she had hardly known him, except years ago at school."[36]

Mrs. Dallon's befuddlement at her daughter's hysteria complicates the scene in a powerful way, and it does this while keeping us at a slight remove from Mary Louise's trauma, a remove that helps us see it more clearly, that allows us, ironically enough, a genuine encounter.

IF WE don't encounter something when we write literature, we're in the realm of kitsch. To my mind, kitsch is, in part, the twentieth century's version of sentimentality, an outgrowth of philosophical idealism and the moral sentiments but an outgrowth that seems less optimistic than stupid, given the realities of daily life. But in our time, kitsch has sources outside of idealism as well. Hallmark-card kitsch is for our grandparents. But that doesn't mean we've abandoned kitsch. We've just updated it with MTV and our it's-all-one-world Internet superhighway patter. Now we've got hip kitsch, rebel kitsch, and "been there, done that" kitsch. No matter. Kitsch is still a way of having emotion—of the warm fuzzy or teenage angsty variety—without addressing anything.

In Manet's famous painting *Olympia,* a nude looks out at her viewer. Her gaze, because it is so direct, feels confrontational. She is stretched out on a couch. In the shadows behind her is a black maid. On the floor below, a kitten and a ball of yarn. The painting created a rather famous stir when it was first shown. In *Mainstreams of Modern Art,* John Canady compares *Olympia* to Canabel's *Birth of Venus,* a painting which he describes as "as erotic a nude as has ever been put on public exhibition"—but one that didn't scandalize the public the way Manet's did.[37] And why not? Presumably because Canabel's image used visual clichés—little putti floating above the nude, studio waves below—in order to figuratively cloak the woman's nakedness and make it acceptable. "When we look at such a painting," writes philosopher Karsten Harries, "we don't really confront anything. . . . The picture itself becomes unimportant; it is merely a stimulus to evoke a mood."[38] *Olympia,* on the other hand, is (in Canaday's words) "not only a representation of reality but a revelation of it."[39] For Manet's contemporaries presumably, a revelation of reality—to *truly* see a nude—was too much: it was vulgar. Better to get what *Birth of Venus* offered—not the object of desire but desire itself. And this is what kitsch is, according to Harries. Kitsch is not an encounter with a thing but with the emotion itself, and since the emotion is in the viewer, kitsch is self-enjoyment, a masturbatory pleasure. This neatly explains both why such work isn't particularly good and also why it is so popular. And it coincides, essentially, with Milan Kundera's definition of kitsch as "the translation of the stupidity of received ideas," that is, the translation of clichés, "into the language of beauty and feeling. It moves us to tears for ourselves, for the banality of what we think and feel."[40]

I present myself as an embarrassing example. One day my mother came home to find me—on a college break—watching TV and tearing up at *Snoopy Come Home,* because, well, Snoopy . . . he hadn't come home. Cute little cartoon voices were singing, "Snooo-ooo-oppy, Snooo-ooo-oopy, come home, Snoopy, come home, come home, come home, come home," and I was a wreck.

TRACK 6.

I was hoping Track 6 would be an original tune. But it's not. Just a quick final verse for Track 5. Please note: I'm not anti-Peanuts. I'm as pro-Snoopy as the next gal. But when it comes to serious literature, kitsch is invariably going to be dissatisfying. We need to get out of ourselves and encounter something else to convey effectively emotion. How does this square with what I said earlier—that our passions and griefs are all we have to offer? Quite well, I hope, because our passions and griefs are about some *thing,* or they should be if our aim is to share them with others.

John Barth apparently once said that emotion in literature is like lovemaking. We want passion, but passion without control is clumsy and unfulfilling. We need virtuosity, but technique without passion is no good. We want passionate virtuosity. And, I'd add, it would be grand if someone (in addition to the author) showed up for the romp in the hay.

Curious Attractions
MAGICAL REALISM'S FATE IN THE STATES

Lɪᴋᴇ ᴀ lot of people, I'd like to write what I like to read. And my early passions were for the so-called magical realists—the deliriously imaginative Gabriel García Márquez, Nikolai Gogol, and Julio Cortázar. Later Steve Stern, Stuart Dybek, and Louise Erdrich. But when I set myself the task of writing this kind of fiction—by which I mean fiction that struck me as fantastic, in all senses of the word—I found myself hobbled by an inability to get my imagination to work in this country. In the end, I set my first novel in Puerto Rico and felt safe to dream what I would. I have family connections to San Juan, but the move to set a novel on the island did fill me with dread. Would people accuse me of cultural colonialism? The artistic equivalent of what has, in fact, been the political history of that island? What right did I have to this material? And so on. Of course, I had to put aside those potential criticisms to write my book. In leaving them behind, another, to me more interesting, question has arisen in its place. Why is it so hard for me to imagine magical realist fiction on my own soil?

One obvious answer is that there aren't many literary models to follow. When it comes to magical realist fiction, the States don't have the same rich tradition as South America with its Borgeses and Mario Vargas Llosas, as Europe with its Bruno Schulzes and Milan Kunderas. But the truth is I don't write consciously from a literary model but from my perception of the world. Granted, my sense of the world is influenced by what I read, but even so, it seems my imagination's domestic recalcitrance has to be about something else. Now part of this "something else" is—I know, I know—a matter for me and my therapist, entirely personal and idiosyncratic, but part, I suspect, isn't, since the paucity of North American literary models suggests that other North American writers are similarly cowed when it comes to letting their imaginations loose within this country's borders.

In her essay, "The Strange History of the American Fantastic," Victoria Nelson points out that it's not that the magical or the fantastic has no place in contemporary North American literature but that it has no place in high art, that it has been relegated to genre literature and other mass culture forms, most notably the movies.[1] In the twentieth century, the exceptions she finds are the literary experiments of the 1950s and 1960s—the works of Donald Barthelme, John Barth, and John Hawkes, among others—and the writing of domestic "minority" writers. She mentions Toni Morrison and Maxine Hong Kingston, but readers of contemporary literature should have no problem adding names to the list: Susan Power, Louise Erdrich, and Amy Tan.

Certainly there are plenty of exceptions to this generalization about North American fiction, but I'll accept it as a starting point so I can ask a question for which I don't yet have an answer. It's a question that comes to me straight from the playgrounds of my youth. It comes in a sneer, a derisive Boston accent: "Spark, what's *your* problem?" I don't have the sociological wherewithal to answer completely the question of why a certain kind of imagination is inimical to the States, but narrow the question down to myself, and I'm on firmer ground. So: What *is* my problem? What's wrong with my imagination that I can't get it to work here? And, while I'm at it, what are the other potential stumbling blocks for the budding North American magical realist?

BUT FIRST I want to explain, in some detail, what kind of imagination I'm talking about. What do I mean, what does anyone mean, by invoking the term *magical realism?* In their introduction to the 1984 anthology *Magical Realist Fiction,* editors David Young and Keith Hollaman write,

> One way to understand "magical realism" is as a kind of pleasant joke on "realism," suggesting as it does a new kind of fiction, produced in reaction to the confining assumptions of realism, a hybrid that somehow manages to combine the "truthful" and

"verifiable" aspects of realism with the "magical" effects we associate with myth, folktales, tall story, and that being in all of us—our childhood self, perhaps—who loves the spell the narrative casts even when it is perfectly implausible. . . . A crucial feature of the term, then, lies in its duality. . . . What this suggests is that the most distinctive aspects of magical realism lie at the point where two different realities intersect, perhaps to collide, perhaps to merge. Familiar oppositions—life and death, waking and sleeping, child and adult, civilized and "savage"—are much at home in this genre, though not necessarily with their differences resolved.[2]

Canadian writer Robert Kroetsch echoes Young and Hollaman when he claims that, with magical realism, "the bargain you make with your reader is quite different from the bargain you make in fantasy. [Magical realism is] not about a uniform fantastic world but about a collision of two worlds."[3]

Bernard Malamud's "The Jewbird" is, then, an example of magical realism. In it, Schwartz, a Jewbird, flies into the New York apartment of Cohen, a frozen food salesman. The Jewbird resembles an aging immigrant Jew; he's a scholar who speaks Yiddish and wants only a nice piece of herring for supper. But he is undoubtedly a bird. He flaps about the apartment and tries to keep his distance from the pet cat.[4] Malamud never tries to explain how an otherwise realistic story can include a figure who is essentially from a fairy tale. A talking bird, after all. Familiar oppositions—man and animal, realistic and fantastic—are not resolved by the story or by the narrator's voice, which expresses no disbelief at the presence of a talking bird in the story.

As a definition of magical realism, the editors of *Magical Realist Fiction* do a good job. They leave me, however, with the question: Why would it be easier to overlap realities in one place than another? And is that all that magical realism is about? Overlapping realities? To answer this, I want to step back to look at the origin of the term to see if there are other ways of understanding magical realism.

IF YOU'RE interested in Latin American fiction, any thorough reading about the term *magical realism* will eventually lead you to an art critic, a novelist, and a literary critic—to Franz Roh, Alejo Carpentier, and Angel Flores. All three are considered to have, at different times and in different countries, coined the term, and this mix-up seems to me to be a classically magical realist phenomenon.

The truth is that in 1925, art critic Franz Roh first used the term *magical realism* in reference to a group of painters, living and working in Germany, who rejected the objectivity of German postimpressionism, the emotionalism and intensity of expressionism.[5] These artists advocated a return to reality, but reality in a new light. They felt that the artist should approach the world of objects as if discovering them for the first time. So originally magical realism wasn't a mix of reality and fantasy, as we have come to think of it, but a way to access the marvelous in the everyday. Indeed, a way to make the natural seem supernatural.[6] In writing about the development of magical realism in the 1930s and 1940s, art critic H. H. Arnason spoke of the "precise realistic presentation of an ordinary scene with no strange or monstrous distortion: the magic arises from a fantastic juxtaposition of elements or events that do not normally belong together."[7]

Roh was talking about visual art when he coined his term, but his definition applies quite well to one of the most famous lines of literature, the opening of Gabriel García Márquez's *One Hundred Years of Solitude:*

> Many years later, as he faced the firing squad, Colonel Aureliano Buendía was to remember that distant afternoon when his father took him to discover ice.[8]

Now, this is a great opening sentence. It starts in the middle of things, it's surprising, a shock of a place for a novel to begin, but what's magical about it is really only one word, the word *discover* as applied to ice. Nothing supernatural here, no woman levitating through the ceiling as there is later in the novel, just a "fantastic juxtaposition of elements."

But when we think of magical realism these days, we tend to think of a definition we could use to describe a story in which a woman levitates through the ceiling or an old shed learns how to fly, and *that* definition didn't come about till the *magical realist* term crossed the ocean and made the leap from visual to literary art. All of which happened in 1927 when Roh's article about visual art was translated into

Spanish and published in José Ortega y Gasset's journal, *Revista de Occidente*.[9] After the translation, the term was used in the literary criticism of Latin America. In the 1930s, critics in Buenos Aires were using the term to describe the work of Kafka and Cocteau.[10] The term wasn't applied to Latin American literature, however, till 1948, when Arturo Uslar Pietri used it in reference to Venezuelan short stories of the 1930s and 1940s. Pietri spoke of these stories as presenting "el hombre como misterio en medio de los datos realistas," man as "a mystery among realistic data."[11]

The sense of what magical realism was changed in 1949 when the Cuban Alejo Carpentier published his novel *El Reino de Este Mundo* (*The Kingdom of This World*). In his introduction to that book, Carpentier introduced his concept of "lo real maravilloso amercano [marvelous American reality]," in which two contrasting views of the world—one rational and modern, the other magical and traditional—were presented as if they were not contradictory. While "lo real maravilloso" used surrealism as a stepping-off point, it was not truly surreal or fantastic. "Lo real maravilloso" isn't another world, Carpentier argued. It isn't a separate reality; rather, it is "an amplification of the scales and categories of reality."[12]

In the body of Carpentier's *El Reino de Este Mundo,* the voodoo beliefs of the Haitian blacks seem no stranger than their horrible enslavement. And, indeed, the strangest part of the novel—concerning the life and death of the megalomaniacal Henri Christophe, a slave who became king of Haiti—is completely true.

Carpentier had been part of the surrealist movement when he lived in Paris, but he'd become disenchanted with it. The art he was practicing in Latin America wasn't an attempt, as surrealism was, to get at the reality beneath everyday reality, the reality that the Western traditions of empiricism and scientific positivism had made people forget. Instead it was, in the words of critic William Spindler, "a representation of a reality modified and transformed by myth and legend."[13]

In Carpentier's novel, the Haitian slaves' leader, a one-armed revolutionary named Macandal, disappears from the community. Presumably he has been killed by the whites, who have discovered his role in a poisoning conspiracy. But no one believes he's dead. Referring to the slave population, Carpentier's narrator says, "They all knew that the green lizard, the night moth, the strange dog, the incredible gannet, were nothing but disguises. As he had the power to take the shape of a hoofed animal, bird, fish or insect, Macandal continually visited the plantations of the Plaine to watch over his faithful and find out if they still had faith in his return. In one metamorphosis or another, the one-armed was everywhere, having recovered his corporeal integrity in animal guise. . . . The dogs did not bark at him; he changed his shadow at will. It was because of him that a Negress gave birth to a child with a wild boar's face."[14]

"Lo real maravilloso" was for Carpentier a uniquely American phenomenon. "What," said Carpentier, "is the history of [Latin] America but a chronicle of marvelous reality?" His words were echoed over three decades later by Gabriel García Márquez when he gave his Nobel Prize speech. In that 1982 address, García Márquez detailed various mad, bloody, and disturbing events in Latin America's history. He spoke, for instance, of General Maximilian Hernández Martínez, who, in a killing orgy, wiped out thirty thousand El Salvadoran peasants and who also, in a more benign mood, covered the street lamps of his city with red paper to combat an epidemic of scarlet fever. Given the region's history, García Márquez said, Latin American writers "have needed to ask little of the imagination, for the major challenge before us has been the want of conventional resources to make our life credible."[15] Magic realism, then, could be seen as a literary form that expresses what life is like in Latin America. The critic Frederic Jameson has said that magical realism doesn't present a reality which needs to be "transfigured by the 'supplement' of a magical perspective but a reality which is already in and of itself magical or fantastic."[16] Alejo Carpentier felt that magical realism was not literary and artificial, as presumably the European equivalents were, but a result of the lives of the Latin American natives, who did not draw a line between the real and the supernatural.[17]

Understood this way, magical realism is an expression of the popular culture, the way the folk see things. Indeed, Carpentier saw magical realism as an ultimately political form, since it preserved an identity otherwise overshadowed by colonialism. Summarizing Carpentier's argument, Spindler concluded, "The strength of Magic Realism in the 'periphery' (Latin America, Africa, the Caribbean) and its comparative weakness in the core (Western Europe, the USA) could be explained by the fact that collective myths acquire greater importance in the creation of new national identities, as well as by the more obvious fact that pre-industrial beliefs still play an important part in the socio-political and cultural lives of developing countries. Magic Realism gives popular culture and magical beliefs the same degree of importance as Western science and rationality. In doing this, it furthers the claims of these groups which hold these beliefs to equality with the modernizing elites which govern them."[18]

If I stop here in my definitions of magical realism and ask again what my imagination's problem is, I can answer. If I trust Alejo Carpentier's definition, I can say that my problem is connected to the lack of a collective mythology in the United States and to my participation in a Western society which valorizes the empirical. I can also see that my initial anxiety about being a cultural impostor has roots in the form, as well as the subject matter, of some of the fiction I've loved. I can imagine a sort of tug-of-war between myself and Carpentier, the toy of *his* experience between us. I've got one leg of the doll, he has the other, and he's shouting, "No, you can't have it. It's mine." And in response I've got the fiction writer's arrogance that says— *sotto voce* maybe—but says, "I can go where I want to go." But even as I say this, I realize I'm going where I don't want to go: into the debate over the politics of the imagination, the question of who gets to imagine what. I have recourse, in defending myself, to Bob Shacochis's angry response to critics of his writing about the Caribbean. "Can you imagine," Shacochis writes, "an Anglo burn victim telling Michael Ondaatje that his brilliant book *The English Patient* is an act of exploitation because he, Ondaatje, is not English but Sri Lankan, and because he has never had serious burns all over his body? Can you imagine a member of the British Parliament dismissing *The Remains of the Day* because it was written by a Japanese immigrant? This point of view would require us all to lock ourselves in our rooms and masturbate. It is perverse. It is obscene. Ultimately, it doesn't matter from what culture, or skin, or gender, the voice of consciousness comes. It only matters that it does come and when it arrives, that we recognize it."[19]

I agree with Shacochis, though his impassioned defense of the writer's right to imagine what he or she will doesn't explain why I don't *want* to leave Carpentier's doll alone and play my game in my own yard. Or course, one reason is that Carpentier's yard—indeed anyone else's yard—is more fascinating than my own, but the real reason is that I can't completely figure out where my own yard is.

In this regard, I think of the struggles of one of my favorite writers,

Memphis-born and -bred Steve Stern. He describes himself as a su-persecular Jew from your typical bowdlerized suburb. His favorite writer, I believe, is Bruno Schulz. For years, as Stern traveled from Tennessee to a commune in Arkansas to a flat in London, he wrote accomplished but unextraordinary fiction. Finally, down on his luck, he returned to Memphis and got a job typing for the Center for Southern Folklore. Among the things he started to transcribe were stories of the Pinch, the Jewish neighborhood that once existed by the river in downtown Memphis. While typing, something clicked for Stern. The material spoke to him—it was *his* material—and he started writing wild, innovative stories about, among other things, a *schlep* of a kid who discovers that on the steamy nights when his neighbors sleep in the local park, he can climb a tree and enter their collective dream, changing their night thoughts at will.[20] As I understand it, it wasn't until Stern discovered the material that would suit his imagination that he was able to write his best work. And to do this, he had to leave his own yard behind, but he didn't have to go too far, since what was required of him was to enter his ancestors' yards. To write magical realism, he had to leave his century but not his hometown. And once he did, he started reading Jewish mysticism, learning Yiddish—accessing, in effect, a mythology for his work.

Presumably, then, there *is* a kind of magical realism that requires some cultural reckoning, and the degree to which one is willing or able to do this is the degree to which one is able to free up one's imagination. This explains, in part, why magical realism has flourished in areas where people need to reclaim their cultural identity and why "minority" writers produce much of the United States's magical realism. In "The Strange History of the American Fantastic," Victoria Nelson writes, "One cannot hold citizenship in two realms at the same time."[21] But, of course, some people can. Indeed, magical realism is, as we've seen, about holding citizenship in two realms, which may explain why, in addition to everything else, it is a popular form for Asian Americans, African Americans, Native Americans, people whose cultural identity puts them in two realms. It may also explain why some North Americans shy away from magical realism. American American is no real opposition. And being, say, a part-Scottish, half-Baptist, Floridian American may mean your sense of cultural identity is too fuzzy to exploit.

Nelson points out that even immigrant writers are affected by the

North American passion for realism. When Isaac Bashevis Singer came to this country, she notes, he was transformed "from a mystic folklorist into a bleak and mordant observer of erotic survivors, real live revenants. . . . In America Singer drastically relocated and secularized the source of what might be called 'wonder'—the supernatural, the irrational, the defiance of natural laws. No longer did he attribute this quality to external reality, as supernatural creatures or magical acts, an integral part of a coherent religious universe, a manifestation of God's inscrutable will; once in America, he relocated it within the human temperament, characteristically expressing itself in the spontaneous, perverse, unpredictable course of amorous adventures."[22]

One might argue that this has more to do with, say, the Holocaust than this country, but we can find other examples of writers who relocated their "source of wonder" when they came to the States. Isabel Allende, for one. Since she moved to San Francisco, her writing has changed. Her new works—*The Infinite Plan* and *Paula*—have little of the magic of *The House of Spirits* or *The Stories of Eva Luna*.

One is tempted to conclude that in the United States, when wonder isn't about a collision of cultures, it is internal or interpersonal. True, for some writers, like Don DeLillo, our commercial culture appears to provide the same wealth of material that Latin America provides for García Márquez, but for many others, it does not. McDonald's and strip malls suck the creativity right out of them.

So, what's a wannabe magical realist to do? Fortunately, Alejo Carpentier's definition of magical realism isn't the only one. Franz Roh's definition, where the artist finds the marvelous in the everyday, describes, I suspect, what most fiction writers imagine they're up to. And there's also the possibility of a magical realism that isn't culturally constructed. There are many kinds of realities, beyond cultural realities, that can be overlapped in fiction. Look at Gogol's "The Nose," with its critique of a stagnating bureaucracy incapable of wonder. Or Kafka, where the waking world and nightmare seem to be one and the same. Look, too, at the formulation of magical realism—the one I haven't yet gotten to—by Angel Flores, where the strange is not necessarily born of a particular community's mythology but of the author's imagination.

Angel Flores is credited with coining the term *magical realism,* but what he really did was popularize the term, since neither Roh's nor Carpentier's definitions seemed to stick in the public consciousness. In 1955, Flores delivered a much maligned but nonetheless influential paper at the Modern Language Association conference.[23] In it, Flores said that the romantic and realistic have always existed side by side in Latin American fiction, but in the twentieth century, there were two significant shifts in how these opposites were handled. One came after World War I. The other in 1935. In looking at the artists of the twenties, Flores noted what art critic Roh had observed in Germany: a number of writers and painters—people like Proust, Kafka, and di Chirico—were reacting against the photorealism of many of the arts and rediscovering symbolism and magical realism. This was a *re*discovery because post–World War I writers could find models for what they were doing in nineteenth-century figures: the Russians Gogol and Dostoevsky, the German romantics Hoffman and the Grimm brothers, and, to some extent, the Americans Poe and Melville. But Angel Flores didn't consider the post–World War I writers magical realists, for their work was, he thought, dependent on atmosphere, mood, and sentiment. They differed from "the cold and cerebral and often erudite storytell[ers]" that flourished in the wake of the 1935 publication of Jorge Luis Borges's collection, *Historia Universal de La Infamia.*[24] "With Borges as pathfinder and moving spirit," Flores writes, "a group of brilliant stylists developed around him."[25] Their work headed in the general direction of magical realism. They were clean, sophisticated, precise writers, interested in style and in surprise. They all subscribed to di Chirico's dictum about art: "What is most of all necessary is to rid art of everything of the known which it has held until now: every subject, idea, thought and symbol must be put aside. . . . Thought must draw so far away from human fetters that things may appear to it under a new aspect, as though they are illuminated by a constellation now appearing for the first time."[26]

Flores noted that magical realist stories often had one element that could not be explained away by logic or psychology and that once the reader accepted that as a "*fait accompli,* the rest [of the story] follows with logical precision."[27] A story like Julio Cortázar's "Letter to a Young Lady in Paris" is a perfect example of this. In it, a man writes to confess something to the woman whose flat he is letting:

> I was going up in the elevator and just between the first and second floors I felt that I was going to vomit up a little rabbit. I

have never described this to you before, not so much, I don't think, from lack of truthfulness as that, just naturally, one is not going to explain to people at large that from time to time one vomits up a small rabbit.[28]

Once you accept the fantastic premise, Cortázar's despairing narrator acts, more or less, as *you* might if you were a neatnik puking bunnies in your friend's apartment.

Echoing Flores, the editors of *Magical Realist Fiction* point out that there are two possible directions for a magical realist story: either it starts with a fantastic premise and then adheres to logic and natural law, as in "Letter to a Young Lady in Paris," or, as in a piece like Borges's "The Aleph," familiar events turn extraordinary in the course of the story.

In "The Aleph," a successful writer named Borges mourns the loss of his love, Beatriz Viterbo. When he visits her old house and pays respects to her family, he falls victim to her cousin, the boring and pompous Carlos Argentino Daneri, who wants to take advantage of Borges's literary expertise and connections. Soon enough, Daneri confesses that the inspiration for his ponderous poem "The Earth" is the Aleph in his basement. An Aleph, he explains to the incredulous Borges, is a point that contains all others. Eventually, Borges descends to the basement and sees for himself. There, in the space of an inch, is, in fact, everything. In looking at the Aleph, Borges sees the whole of the "unimaginable universe." He lists off what he sees for the reader: I saw *this* and I saw *that*. Toward the end of his lengthy, miraculous description, he writes,

I saw all the ants on the planet; I saw a Persian astrolabe; I saw in the drawer of a writing table (and the handwriting made me tremble) unbelievable, obscene, detailed letters, which Beatriz had written to Carlos Argentino; I saw a monument I worshipped in the Chacarita cemetery; I saw the rotted dust and bones that had once deliciously been Beatriz Viterbo; I saw the circulation of my own dark blood; I saw the coupling of love and the modification of death; I saw the Aleph from every point and angle, and in the Aleph I saw the earth and in the earth the Aleph and in the Aleph the earth; I saw my own face and my own bowels; I saw your face.[29]

Here you have a story that has overlapping realities galore—not only do the fantastic and real overlap, but reader and character and writer and narrator overlap. What's more, the magic in this passage comes not only from the bizarre Aleph but from the extraordinary listing of things that we can imagine but that we can't imagine seeing simultaneously or, in some cases, can't imagine actually seeing with our own eyes. Ants, yes. All the ants on the planet, no. We can see our blood but never our dark blood, and so on.

In "The Aleph" and "Letter to a Young Lady in Paris," the natural and supernatural are presented on the same level of reality. If anything, the supernatural is made to seem natural, which is, if you think about it, the direct opposite of Franz Roh's original definition of magical realism. According to Alejo Carpentier, as we've seen, this presentation of the rational and magical as if they aren't contradictory is a result of popular culture, the way things are perceived in Latin America and, perhaps, in other "periphery" communities. The antinomy may not, however, even need that explanation, may not need the support of a collective mythology. Sometimes the imagination is freestanding, and, as William Spindler puts it, "the total freedom and creative possibilities of writing are exercised by the author, who is not worried about convincing the reader."[30]

In his story, Borges tries to explain the Aleph to himself, but his answers never dispute the idea that something like an Aleph could exist. Indeed, while expressing his amazement, Borges works to "convince" his readers in other, visceral ways that the Aleph is real. In the end, Borges never has recourse to a rational, a psychological, or a cultural explanation for the "unreal" aspects of his story. He doesn't use—as so much genre fiction does—the "it was all a dream" addendum.

Interestingly, Nikolai Gogol, in early drafts of "The Nose," employed several dream escape clauses, even using the word *dream* in the story's subtitle.[31] As published, "The Nose" is about a Petersburg barber who finds a civil servant's nose in his morning bread—a knobby thing right there in the center of the loaf. More or less simultaneously, a civil servant (shaved by the barber earlier in the week) wakes to find his nose missing. A terrible humiliation. Made worse by the fact that later the civil servant spots his nose gallivanting about town and pretending to a higher rank in the civil service than the man on whose face he belongs. In his first draft, Gogol ended "The Nose" with the line, "Everything that has happened here occurred to Major Kovalev in a dream, and when he woke up, he was so overjoyed that he jumped out of bed, ran up to the mirror, and seeing that everything was right in place, began dancing in his nightshirt a combination of a mazurka and a quadrille around the room."[32] In the end, Gogol cut these lines and left the story's absurdity unexplained. Indeed, he emphasized that the absurdity was not a dream. Kovalev, the civil servant, on discovering a flat spot in the center of his face, "pinches himself to see whether he was still asleep: no, he did not appear to be asleep."[33] The story further discourages attempts to explain its own mysteries. Kovalev's notions about how he lost his nose prove to be misguided, his accusations of a woman he's been courting embarrassing.

Gabriel García Márquez's short story "A Very Old Man with Enormous Wings" makes similar fun of our need to label, to name the unnameable. When a very old man with enormous wings lands in the yard of Pelayo and his wife, Elisenda, people think of him as a devil, an angel, a Nordic sailor, a nightmare, or a circus sideshow act. Eventually they feel he is a nuisance, because they can't figure him out. They can't say what he *is.* Then, another curiosity arrives in town, a woman who has been "changed into a spider for having disobeyed her parents."[34] Unlike the silent old man, she is happy to talk about her troubles. "A spectacle like that," confesses García Márquez's narrator, "full of so much human truth and with such a fearful lesson, was bound to defeat without even trying that of a haughty angel who scarcely deigned to look at mortals."[35] But the narrator's tongue is clearly in his cheek, for he leads us to feel there's something grotesque about the spider woman, something equally unappealing about those who appreciate her but fail to wonder at the infinitely patient old man who is kept in a chicken coop by Pelayo and Elisenda.

ACCESSING THE imagination—whether that imagination is freestanding or culturally constructed—seems to me to be the first challenge for a magical realist. There are others—a host of potential problems for dabblers in this form. The most notable one, I think, is trickery. In an interview, García Márquez once said of *One Hundred Years of Solitude,* "Since I knew it was written with all the tricks and artifices under the sun, I knew I could do better even before I wrote it."[36] Good God, one thinks. Really? But one knows what he's talking about: even magic can become stale.

Borges once said, "I feel that the kind of stories you get in *The Aleph* or *Ficciones* are becoming rather mechanical and that people expect that kind of thing from me. So that I feel as if I were a kind of high fidelity, a kind of gadget, no? A kind of factory producing stories about mistaken identity, about mazes, about tigers, about mirrors, about people being somebody else, or about all men being the same man or one man being his own mortal foe."[37]

In magic realism, we want the magic to knock us off our seats because it's so fabulous, but we also want the magic to have a purpose, a reason for being—hopefully, a reason that will address the heart's concerns.

Magic, even the word, makes us think of childhood, and part of our pleasure in magic realism is related to the childhood pleasure of being told a wild tale. That said, we are not children and are bound to be frustrated if our magic realism has the reductive morality, the emotional simplicity of a fairy tale. In a rather snotty article in the *New Criterion*, Martha Bayles complains about Toni Morrison, arguing that Morrison's embracing of magical realism has led her to embrace a "willful romanticism, which, in the context of black America, leads to the corollary that the most marginal people are the least corrupted by the false values of the dominant white society. [Morrison] assumes that the lower a character's social status, the higher his mythic consciousness."[38] Even if you completely disregard Bayles's analysis of Morrison, she does point to a danger of magical realism: you can get so smitten with the folk, the magic, that you forget that what makes magical realism powerful is its often disturbing blend of the fantastic and the real. As much as magical realism makes demands on your imagination, it requires your thoughtful perceptions of the "real" world.

As a literary choice, magical realism may be a bit cowardly—a move to external exoticism as a way to avoid internal complexity . . . or internal pain. I, at least, have been guilty of this. After I finished my first novel, I went to Barbados to do research for a second book. People always laugh knowingly when I say I went to the Caribbean for research, but it wasn't a happy time. The visit came just after a death in the family, and I spent a good deal of my down time—my hours away from the Jews I was interviewing—alone in a rum punch haze.

One day, while I was waiting for a local bus to start its drive to a northern pottery village, a Rastafarian started taunting me, fairly viciously. In the midst of his diatribe about what the white girl be, I thought, "Why am I doing this?" It wasn't as if I lacked for material in my own life. Why had I come all this way to find a story? I sat heavily on the bus. With all my heart, I wanted to skip the ride into the mountains, to go back to my hotel room and sleep for days, until it was time for my flight home. But to go home in my fiction? I couldn't do that. Perhaps because some of what the Rastafarian was yelling seemed true. Certainly because my own life seemed, at that point, too painful.

Not surprisingly, I had a lot of trouble working on my Barbados novel until I broke down and reconceived it so it addressed the very material I was trying to avoid. So, while one definition of magical realism frees you up to imagine what you will, it doesn't give you every freedom; it doesn't give you the freedom to ignore your own heart.

So where does all this leave the North American writer who is interested in magical realism? Or where does it leave me, since I started by saying I couldn't answer for anyone but myself? Well, with some sense of why I've left the States to write my fiction and a conviction that I shouldn't need to do that, even if I'll probably keep at it. Such hypocrisy deserves to be punished, I think, for I'm really right where I started: blinking at the work I like and considering the work I want to write, thinking, for example, of Julio Cortázar's story "Axolotl," where a man finds himself curiously drawn to the axolotls in the zoo. Daily, this man goes to look at these Mexican salamanders till one day he finds he's a salamander looking at a man visiting the zoo.[39] Me? I'm also looking at what I'm curiously drawn to and finding myself in the uncomfortable position of having to look back at myself.

Aspects of the Short Novel

I IMAGINE most writers are visited by late-night flashes of insight. Ideas so fabulous—so perfect in the connections they make, the problems they resolve—that there's no need to actually get up, brave the cold of the floor, find a pencil and write them down. How could anyone forget such good ideas? But laziness, it turns out, is bad for great ideas. So is daylight, which has a transmogrifying effect on nocturnal discoveries, causing them to vanish or appear—suddenly, unrecognizably—stupid. Here's one of my late-night realizations. Not an idea really, but a desire that came to me, with some ferocity, during the writing of my last novel, a six-hundred-pager, a real doorstop of a book. I would—I should—try to write a short novel.

Not much of a thought, it's true, but I'd been rereading some of my slim favorites—William Maxwell's *So Long, See You Tomorrow,* Lorrie Moore's *Who Will Run the Frog Hospital?* Chinua Achebe's *Things Fall Apart,* and Norman Maclean's *A River Runs Through It*—and felt the need for a diet. Still, the desire struck me as somewhat specious, as if past midnight, my head sprang up from the pillow, and I fervently declared, "I'll write an eighteen-page story." Who, after all, picks the length before the subject?

Recently, in doing a quick survey of critical writing about the novella, I realized my urge to write a short piece was about something deeper, about something I intended, but failed, to do in my longer work, something a longer work might not be able to do as well as a shorter one. More about that later. For now, suffice it to say that short novels and novellas describe more than a page count, they describe a form, and in wanting to write a short novel, I'd been wanting some of the power of that form.

Before I begin: an explanation of my title. "Aspects of the Short Novel." Stolen, as you may know, from E. M. Forster. His book *Aspects of the Novel* consists of a series of lectures which Forster gave at Trinity College in 1927. Forster says he chose the word *aspects* because "it means both the different ways we can look at a novel and the different ways a novelist can look at his work."[1] The aspects Forster addressed provided the titles for each of his lectures: "The Story," "People," "Plot," "Fantasy," "Prophecy," and "Pattern and Rhythm." Following him, I've divided my thoughts on short novels into seven sections: "The Miniskirt," "Goldilocks," "Philosophy 101," "Transparent Buildings," "Bummer Fiction," "The Levitating Mailman," and "Enough about Me, What Do You Think of Me?"

The Miniskirt

FIRST, THE miniskirt, which raises the whole question of length and allows me to do a bit of show-and-tell. Today's object for display, my graduate school T-shirt, originally black, now gray. On the front, it reads, "Iowa Writers Workshop 1936/1986." And on the back, these five lines:

a. I think this is really two T-shirts.
b. I think you should expand this T-shirt into a sweatshirt.
c. I don't think this T-shirt quite comes together.
d. Nothing happens in this T-shirt.
e. I don't think this works as a T-shirt.

I'm concerned here with the second piece of advice, which I always misremember as "I think this T-shirt really wants to be a dress." I see my subconscious is line editing my T-shirt. Sweatshirt—*that* doesn't make sense. The idea is that the T-shirt should be longer, not thicker. The T-shirt should be a dress. Perhaps you've had this sartorial advice applied to one of your own short stories. In workshops, says novelist Susan Kenney, we reflexively make this suggestion when the author has too many pages. It is not, she says, really "an aesthetic decision, but on account of lack of discipline."[2] I am struck, in this regard, by how many of my undergraduate students want to conclude their program of college writing classes with a semester of independent study in which they write a novella. They haven't read any novellas—save, perhaps, *Heart of Darkness*—but the impulse is clear enough. They will segue into the novel with the novella. After all the page count isn't *that* daunting. Most critics put it somewhere between fifteen and fifty thousand words. Which means, if you're using Courier type, sixty to two hundred pages. But for students, often uninclined as writers to getting to the point, the urge to write a novella may not make much sense. A general truth in the fashion world: it's much harder to pull off a miniskirt than a dress.

As with skirt lengths, so with stories; the paramount question is one of appropriateness. None of us—at dinner parties or in our writing—want to be accused of going on too long. "Enough talk," the boys at my high school used to bark during morning assembly when they grew tired of a speaker. I'm still amazed that there was no punishment for this sort of insistence on brevity. But, perhaps, they were doing the speaker a favor. In *The Writing of Fiction,* Edith Wharton tells us, "A novelist who does not know when his story is finished, but goes on stringing episode to episode after it is over, not only weakens the effect of the conclusion, but robs of significance all that has gone before."[3] Page count, she notes, will be determined by subject, and one needn't concern oneself in advance with the abstract question of length. That said, she writes, "In the act of composition, [the writer] must never cease to bear in mind that one should always be able to say of a novel: 'It might have been longer,' never: 'It need not have been so long.'"[4] The important question, then, is not how long something should be but how much development a subject requires.

So how much space does your subject require? Can you know in advance? Be taught? Perhaps it is more of an instinct, the same instinct that tells you how to time a joke. An instinct that is based on a sense of the qualitative difference between material that is right for a short story and material that is right for a novel.

Goldilocks

ECONOMICAL, FOCUSED, and dense, short stories usually concentrate on a limited number of psyches and actions, often structuring themselves around a single event and aiming for a single emotional realization. Novels tend to be longer works of fiction that allow for more of everything the short story has: more characters, plots, and plot developments; more settings; access to more consciousnesses. Rather than having one epiphany, it has a series of lesser crises and attendant realizations which culminate in a final climax and epiphany. The novella or short novel falls somewhere in between these two extremes in both length and breadth. Which is to say, novellas and short novels have some of the compression of a short story, some of the expansion of a novel. They can have more characters than short stories and can sustain a deeper and longer exploration of those characters, but they can't have the multiple plotlines, settings, and characters of a *War and Peace.* The novella is Goldilocks form, not too much this and not too much that but just right.

Just right for what? Before I answer, I should acknowledge that so far I've been using the terms *short novel* and *novella* interchangeably. Many critics do, but writers as various as Steven Millhauser and Henry James make sharp distinctions between the two. Millhauser thinks of the novella as an outgrowth of the short story, having only a "dim and accidental" relation to the novel, while he considers the short novel, as its very name suggests, to be a next-door neighbor of the novel.[5] Henry James defined the novella, or "nouvelle," as it was called in his day, as a form—eighteen to forty-five thousand words long—perfect for the working out of a single idea, for following an emotional arc.[6] For him, it needn't be grounded in the social milieu, though short novels—eighty to a hundred thousand words long—depended on social observation. In *Writing a Book That Makes a Difference,* Philip Gerard writes that "a novella commonly follows the fortunes of a single character through a limited time in a circumscribed locale, focusing on a central action. In conceptual terms, it is much more of a long short story than a short novel."[7] Indeed, the definition sounds rather like a definition for a short story. Still, plenty of novellas can be described this way: James's *nouvelles* or Thomas Mann's *A Death in Venice.* But the four books I mentioned earlier—by Lorrie Moore, William Maxwell, Norman Maclean, and Chinua Achebe—are hardly circumscribed in their action or time frame, so I should say that I am primarily concerned here with longer novellas and short novels.

Given this caveat, back to my question: exactly what are novellas just right for?

There's not, it turns out, a great deal of definitive critical writing about modern and contemporary novellas composed in English or even Russian. The form has always seemed diffuse to critics, especially when compared to the German *novelle,* French *nouvelle,* or Renaissance novella. That said, those who do hazard generalizations focus on the form's beauty, its ability to explore a single philosophical or moral idea, and its usefulness for parables, fables, or stories that tend to archetype.

Howard Nemerov begins his interesting essay "Composition and Fate in the Short Novel" by writing,

> What are short novels? For the writer who is by habit of mind a novelist they must represent not simply a compression but a corresponding rhythmic intensification, a more refined criterion of relevance than the one he usually enjoys, an austerity and economy perhaps somewhat compulsive in the intention itself. For the writer who habitually thinks in short stories—a bad habit, by the way—the challenge is probably greater: he will have to think about a fairly large space which must be filled, not with everything [Nemerov's complaint against the novelist] but with something definite which must be made to yield in a quite explicit way its most reserved and recondite ranges of feeling; he will have to think, for once, of design and not merely of plot.[8]

In the essay's subsequent paragraph, Nemerov writes that the novella form has a tradition of producing masterpieces. Initially he accounts for this by noting that novellas—too long for magazines, too short for books—aren't particularly marketable. True enough. But the masterpiece tradition may depend more on what Nemerov notes in his first paragraph, on the necessity not just for compression, relevance, and economy—which we expect from a short story—but for "rhythmic intensification" and not just for plot—which we expect from most fiction—but for "design." Of course, we see rhythmic intensification and design in shorter and longer fiction, but Nemerov's definition *emphasizes* these qualities, qualities that appeal—as E. M. Forster might have it—not to our curiosity but our aesthetic sense.

Aspects of the Short Novel •

Nemerov comes up with a definition that says, effectively, that the novella is, by its very nature, beautiful. Sure, you might argue, but isn't this true of a story? a novel? And the answer is no. We don't really talk about beauty when we *define* the novel and short story, even if we hope our own efforts will be lovely. As Arnold B. Sklare, editor of *The Art of the Novella,* says, the problem of balancing the novella's complexity with its unity forces the writer to consider the very "nature of the beautiful, its essential characteristics, and the tests by which it may be judged and related to the human mind."[9]

WHY ELSE might the form lend itself to masterpieces? Perhaps because it concerns itself not only with beauty but with ideas. Of course, so do stories and novels, but repeatedly critics remark on the philosophical bent of novellas, their shadowy didacticism. Ronald Paulson, in his preface to *The Modern Novelette,* speaks of the short form as "a better medium than the novel for the stark contrast desired by the reformer or the moralist," best for stories where one wants to make a "situation exemplary" of some already held idea.[10] And Nemerov writes, "The most striking element shared by almost all the great pieces in this genre is their outright concentration upon traditional problems of philosophy, the boldness of their venture into generality, the evidence they give of direct and profound moral concern."[11] To understand his point, it might be helpful to know that Nemerov thinks the novelist proceeds by inductive reasoning while the short novelist proceeds by deductive reasoning. Which is to say, the short novelist picks a particular story or image or event that will allow him or her to explore an already held idea. Writing, by this definition, isn't discovery, exactly. "In general," says Paulson in his introduction to *The Modern Novelette,* "the novelette has no room for searching about; it must find a striking economic correlative and present it."[12]

Whether Nemerov's observation is true or not, it does seem to touch on the sense we have with many short works of a burrowing into a single construct rather than a gathering up of several ideas. The single construct, then, has a way of opening up, as Nemerov promises, into larger ideas.

Consider, in this regard, Norman Maclean's *A River Runs Through It,* which uses fly fishing as its "striking economic correlative." Through it, Maclean talks explicitly about fly fishing and family, implicitly about the code of the Western world and the limitations of that code. He talks about religion, grace, and salvation. Maclean's novella isn't particularly focused in terms of action or even essential characters. But it does limit its central metaphor, which, in turn, determines everything: the scenes the author will depict, the way in which characters will be portrayed (which is to say, fishing or about to go fishing or returning from fishing or talking about fishing). Wallace Stegner holds that fishing even accounts for the novella's apparently random structure and its abrupt and powerful end, where we learn of Maclean's brother's death.[13]

Of the days when he was completing *A River Runs Through It*, Norman Maclean once said, "I was almost afraid to sleep, afraid I'd lose the connections as it came together."[14] Reading the book, one understands Maclean's fear. It's work to get from the particulars of fly-fishing to general ideas and eventually to grace, work to expect that the reader will follow along, understand, or even accept the links. Could a shorter work have done this? I don't think so. "I love," says writer Steve Stern of the novella form, "the idea of fitting the big genie into the little bottle." Try to stuff Maclean's genie into a smaller container, and something would be left out—a leg, two arms, and redemption. And a longer work, could it have sustained the connections? Or would what feels true in the novella come to seem false? Fly-fishing is a revealing metaphor in the context of Maclean's particular story. But had Maclean's angle of vision or chosen subject been different, the metaphor might have shrunk rather than expanded the reader's sense of the world.

ONE SIDE effect of novellas' relative brevity is that they are necessarily disengaged from some aspects of reality. Now, this is always true with writing. "Your life makes movements," says Maclean, "that have no artistic merit."[15] You never tell the whole story. You pick and choose. The writer always leaves something out. What's left out, of course, changes the nature of what's left in. Shorn of a social milieu (in the case of Henry James) or simply narrative and psychological complication, novellas—particularly if they are, as Howard Nemerov argues, Philosophy 101 in fictional garb—can tend to archetype, allegory, or parable. There are plenty of exceptions to this statement, but Hemingway's *The Old Man and the Sea* is a rather obvious example of its truth, as are Tolstoy's short novels. In a work like Thomas Mann's *Death in Venice* or Joseph Conrad's *Heart of Darkness*, we see how the authors' insistence on certain qualities in Aschenbach, Tadzio, and Kurtz makes the characters seem archetypal. Even a more contemporary novel like Lorrie Moore's *Who Will Run the Frog Hospital?* makes use of this tendency in the short form. She refers to the frogs of her title as representing "the mythic aspect of what I was trying to do."[16]

Transparent Buildings

PART OF what I love about short novels is that they feel substantial and yet their architecture announces itself. They are transparent buildings, floor joists and supporting beams exposed. The condensed novel, notes Steve Stern, who has published many, "has dramatic weight, an intensity, part of which relates to being able to contain them in your mind."[17] This makes me think of how I always study maps when I visit a new city. I want the pleasure of the unknown along with a sense of design, and this is exactly what a short novel provides. And a short novel's ability to do this relates to its focus, its insistence on limitations.

Steven Millhauser's 115-page novella, *The Little Kingdom of J. Franklin Payne,* is about a cartoonist. It starts with the night when J. Franklin Payne, touched with a bit of moon madness, leaves his regular nighttime haunt, his attic study, to walk on the roof of his house. The story then goes back in time, tracing Payne's life through his youth and marriage before bringing us up to the morning after Franklin's moonlight escapade and continuing on. We see Franklin moving with his wife to New York, where he works as a newspaper cartoonist. We meet Payne's best friend, Max, later a business partner of sorts, still later a lover to Payne's wife. And throughout we see Payne's obsessive commitment to his craft.

After the first chapter, Millhauser's story is essentially chronological, and the entire narrative centers on the conflict that plagues so many of Millhauser's characters, a conflict best summed up by Yeats's assertion that "The intellect of man is forced to choose / Perfection of the life, or of the work."[18] Millhauser's character picks art and loses, as a result, his wife and, in the end, his mind.

The story is focused by its basic conflict but achieves unity through a careful use of a central metaphor introduced in the first long sentence of the novella's second chapter:

When Franklin summoned up his childhood in Plains Farms, Ohio, he always remembered three things: the warm, sunbaked smell of the tire that hung from the branch of the sweet-gum tree, the opening in the backyard hedge that led out into the tall meadow grass where he was forbidden to go, and the sound of his father's voice counting slowly and gravely in the darkened kitchen as he bent over the piece of magic paper under the light of the enlarger.[19]

The darkroom reference is followed by a long description of the pleasure of seeing a photographic print develop. Something out of nothing. A black room, white paper, a light (a round globe, distinctly moonlike), and then the magic of the image. The actual memory returns throughout the novella. In his study, with the moon shining above, Payne himself is something of a negative, lit by light, transforming the magic paper before him. Even the memory of the father's steady counting connects to the novella's frequent references to clocks, time, and efficiency. At the story's close, Franklin has worked himself into exhaustion, rejecting time-saving devices so he can hand draw each still for his secret animation project. In the process, Franklin has also worked himself thoroughly into his imagination, forcing reality to recede. In the book's last scene, Franklin arranges a private, attic-studio screening for his extraordinary final work of animation. There, he is visited by everyone who has abandoned him: his wife and best friend and also the dead, most notably his father, "giving off a sweet, disturbing odor of lilies." Back among the living, Franklin's father raises and lowers "the extended index finger of his right hand, counting silently as he watched the screen."[20]

Millhauser's novella's power is directly connected to what is left out. Irving Howe, in his preface to *Classics of Modern Fiction: Eight Short Novels,* writes, "In the short novel, we are almost always aware of the strong executive hand of the writer, molding and shaping, cutting and tightening: he must adhere to a strict standard of relevance when deciding what can be included. As compensation, however, he often achieves a clearer narrative design than the novelist does."[21] In *The Little Kingdom of J. Franklin Payne,* there is a lot one might want to know. More, say, about Cora or about Franklin's other friends. Indeed, Millhauser notes that if the piece *were* a novel, it would *have* to look at Franklin's erotic life and his marriage.[22] But the power of this form is in, as Steve Stern says of the novella in general, "the single, focused theme that's unrelenting."[23]

A note: it is the focused theme, all the symbols and associations that have to do with the work's central concept—not the limitation in action—that creates the power. Off the top of my head, I can think of two short novels—Mario Vargas Llosa's *Who Killed Palomino Malero?* and Abigail Thomas's *An Actual Life*—that are focused in terms of event, character, and setting but not theme or central metaphor and don't have, partially for this reason, a strong sense of design or even dramatic weight. They're short novels but don't partake explicitly in any of the special qualities of the form.

Of course, it's hard to choose an image or moment that contains a complex theme effectively and then play the theme for all its worth, to let a moment in a darkroom contain a whole life, or, if we turn to Lorrie Moore's second novel, to let a single painting contain a work's core.

Lorrie Moore's *Who Will Run the Frog Hospital?* has two narrative lines. In the novel's opening two pages, Berie Carr is in Paris with her husband. She is eating brains, for memory, for a flashback, and we see, right away, why she might not want to be in the present. Her marriage is ailing, and although Berie's punning away about her husband, she tells us, "The affectionate farce I make of him ignores the ways I feel his lack of love for me."[24] On the novel's third page, Moore shifts to memory and has Berie say, "When I was a child, I tried hard for a time to split my voice."[25] The notion of a split voice is one of the book's metaphors, accounting, in part, for the construction of the book, in which the Parisian present frames the central story about Berie's adolescent friendship with a girl named Sils. The narrative focuses on the summer of 1972, when Berie and Sils were fifteen and working at an amusement park called Storyland. Attractive Sils works as Cinderella, Berie as a ticket taker. The girls lunch on Memory Lane, hang out with Little Bo Peep. The summer is punctuated by Sils's pregnancy and Berie's scheme to steal Storyland money to help pay for Sils's abortion. In the end, Berie is caught and sent away to a Christian camp, and the girls drift apart. We see them, once more, when Berie returns to town for a high school reunion. Along the way, we also get a rather detailed portrait of Berie's family, her parents, her brother, and her ill-fated foster sister. But the focus is on the female friendship.

"I wanted," says Moore, " to write about that time in girls' lives when they are almost amphibious, before they have entered the world."[26] Amphibious. Like a frog. In two worlds at once. Which her book is, with its two separate narrative lines. The word points, too, to the novel's title, borrowed from a Nancy Mladenoff painting, a work that, in its black and white form, prefaces the novel and organizes the book every bit as tightly as Millhauser's darkroom memory organizes J. Franklin Payne. In the painting's foreground, there are two frogs, described in the novel as "two wounded frogs, one in a splint, one with a bandage tied around its eye: they looked like frogs who'd been kissed and kissed roughly, yet stayed frogs."[27] In the background are two whispering girls, dressed up, it seems, as boys or Robin Hoods or princes. The painting has a narrative purpose in the book. Sils, we are told, paints, and she is responsible for the painting, which illustrates an event in Berie and Sils's childhood. The friends used to bandage up frogs who had been hurt by the BB guns of neighborhood boys. The Mladenoff painting provides more than the book's title, though, and more than a bit of action for the book. It provides the central imagery. Both girls work at Storyland—an amusement park, a world of fairy tales—and the painting, of course, recalls the myth of kissing frogs and having them turn into princes. Of course, in Moore's hands, this is something of a warped fairy tale, because both these frogs are damaged (actually damaged by boys) and in need of help. The girls in this book *do* kiss men, but those men never turn princely. If anything, it is the girls in the background of the painting, in Berie's past, who are princes, at least when they are together.

Bummer Fiction

IN REVIEWING Lorrie Moore's *Who Will Run the Frog Hospital?* for the *New York Times Book Review*, Caryn James said that she found the end a bit rushed, but then she added that perhaps it was just as well; it might "have been unbearable to look longer."[28] An author might be offended by such criticism or feel she was in good company. Edith Wharton said that Shakespeare's *Macbeth* was "as long as the subject warranted and the nerves of his audience could stand."[29]

When I first started to think about the subject of short novels, I made a list of some of my favorites. Beyond the ones I've already mentioned, the list included Marguerite Duras's *The Lover,* Leo Tolstoy's *The Death of Ivan Ilych,* A. S. Byatt's *The Conjugal Angel,* Steve Stern's *A Wedding Jester,* and Thomas Mann's *A Death in Venice.* And then I asked myself what qualities these works shared. I didn't come up with much, save for obsession and loneliness. Then other titles sprang to my mind: Kafka's *The Metamorphosis;* Henry James's *A Beast in the Jungle, Aspern Papers,* and *The Turn of the Screw;* Carson McCullers's *The Ballad of the Sad Café;* Ian McEwan's *Black Dogs;* Steven Millhauser's *August Eschenberg;* Philip Roth's *Goodbye, Columbus;* Fyodor Dostoevsky's *Notes from Underground.* Bummer fiction, as we used to say in graduate school. Real downers.

Literary fiction, in general, is dark, but the short novel's focus on loneliness and obsession seems to me to be connected to Wharton's comment about *Macbeth.* Certain subjects may work best when they are extended, longer than a short story so we can truly feel the madness in the obsession, the pain in the loneliness, but not so long that the obsession irritates and the loneliness overwhelms. Howard Nemerov goes so far as to say that short novels—"suggestively allied in simplicity and even in length with the tragedies of antiquity"—may be *the* tragic form for modern fiction writers.[30]

Levitating Mailman

AS AN oxymoronic form, compressed yet extended, economical yet large, the short novel may lend itself to other dualities, may be particularly good for collapsing fact and fiction. Earlier, I said that I thought you could do something in a short novel that I hadn't managed to do in my own long novel. Originally, I had wanted my long work to be a magical realist story, dependent on folkloric figures in the Jewish and Barbadian tradition. But as my book unfolded that didn't happen. Characters I'd conceived as archetypes rounded out, the whole book took another turn. I couldn't pull off what I'd intended.

And what I'd intended was something like what Steve Stern does in *The Wedding Jester.* In this novella, a down-on-his-luck writer, student of Jewish folklore, and general cynic accompanies his mother to a Catskills wedding. There, while standing under the wedding canopy, the virginal bride is possessed by a dybbuk, the malevolent spirit of a dead borscht belt comedian. The borscht belt comedians were notoriously crude, so you can imagine what starts to come out of the lovely bride's mouth. As local expert on Jewish arcana, the writer is called on to perform an exorcism. The novella is funny, a wild piece made even more powerful if you know some things about Jewish mysticism, particularly that the easiest way to die is supposedly through "the kiss of death." The writer of Stern's story kisses the young woman, after whom he has lusted, however inappropriately, throughout the story, and, in the process, his soul trades places with the borscht belt comic's. The final pages of the story are told from the point of view of a disembodied soul, perhaps a year after the wedding, when, readers well versed in Jewish mysticism will realize, he is in "the storehouse of souls" in Upper Gan Eden, a realm of the afterlife.

Steve Stern says that, for him, the "balance between conventional fiction and fable is much easier in a shorter than in a larger piece because the parameters are fixed. In a longer work, I don't think you can straddle two worlds as easily." To illustrate, he uses the metaphor of chewing gum: stretch it and eventually it starts to sag.[31] The novel begins to seem contrived.

The work of, say, Gabriel García Márquez might seem instantly to disprove Stern's point unless we apply it more narrowly—perhaps to writers who don't experience reality as "magical," to writers who perceive a true disconnect between fact and fantasy, who don't think of a levitating mailman as an ordinary occurrence; writers who nonetheless want their own work to bridge the gap between this world and that.

Now might be a good time to mention that I've been using the word *novella,* so far, in terms of its most recent meaning, that is, to refer to medium-length prose narratives written in the nineteenth, twentieth, and twenty-first centuries. Before that, the term was used, but somewhat differently, for the Renaissance novella and the German *novelle. Novella* is an Italian word which means "little new thing." Originally the understanding of the word had nothing to do with length and everything to do with newness. What was new, when the term was coined, was a more realistic depiction of experience. So even though I've made a point of saying that novellas can be good for parables, the term originally suggested one could be freed from the constraints of presenting experience as parabolic. That said, as the novella term aged, it lost some of its definition. The romantics restored some of the abandoned literary conventions, though those conventions have been changed, most notably, secularized, over the years.[32] None of this is all that significant for writers, I think, save to point out that there is something in the history of the word that suggests the tension between romanticism and realism, a tension that certain contemporary writers have exploited.

Enough about Me, What Do You Think of Me?

ONE LAST quote from Howard Nemerov, and it is about self-consciousness:

> I am tempted to think that the characteristic economy of the short novel, its precisely defined space, the peculiar lucidity and simplicity of its internal forms . . . tends to involve the artist more overtly than usual in trying to expound by fantasies what he himself is and what he is doing in his art.[33]

In other words, short novels often fall into that category so useful for lit crit classes: art about art. They're aware of themselves as written, often serving as a metaphor for or comment on the writing process. It's true that several exemplars of the form are notably self-conscious. *The Turn of the Screw* and *Heart of Darkness* are both stories that are about their telling. In the Henry James, a ghost story is told to us by someone who has heard it from someone else who is quoting an account written by yet another person. *Heart of Darkness* is a story about Kurtz told by Marlow to someone else, who tells the story to us. The piece is framed by a question about storytelling: how it is possible to tell the terrible tale of Kurtz to Kurtz's girlfriend and thus to all of us who have not experienced "the horror, the horror."

And more contemporary examples: Steven Millhauser's cartoonist is, in certain ways, a stand-in for the writer. (Not the actual author but the writer in general.) Lorrie Moore's short novel takes place in Storyland. Literally, metaphorically, since all fiction takes place in Storyland. Moore's narrator takes pains to say her childhood had "no narrative," and her hometown was "just a space with some people in it."[34] But, Berie Carr tells us, as she enters into an extended flashback, "one can tell a story anyway. One can get a running start, then begin, do it, and be done." And then, of course, Moore's book does just that.

A short novel that points to the fact of its creation even more explicitly is William Maxwell's *So Long, See You Tomorrow*. The first half of Maxwell's book is autobiographical, recounting two events from Maxwell's small-town boyhood: his mother's death and a local murder. Early on, Maxwell describes how he and another boy, Cletus, used to play on the frame of the house that Maxwell's father was building with his new wife. In the book, each night, when the boys part, they call out to one another, "So long, see you tomorrow." This ritual is cut short when Cletus's father murders his mother's lover. Not long after, Cletus and his mother leave town. Some years later, Maxwell's family moves to Chicago, and one day, at his new high school, Maxwell passes Cletus in the hallway and fails to greet him. Maxwell feels guilty then, guilty decades later, and the book represents, in some ways, Maxwell's effort to atone. The second half of Maxwell's book is an imaginative reconstruction of the lives of the murdered man and the murderer, an effort to understand what happened. Some things, Maxwell tells us, once they are done, can't be undone. Like his mother's death. Like a murder. But the very writing of the book suggests that some things, once done, can be undone.

Because of this setup, imagination and its potentially healing power are central to the book. This is underscored by an image that works, like the painting in Moore's story, the darkroom in Millhauser's story, and fly-fishing in Maclean's story, to thematically focus and organize the entire piece. The image is of Alberto Giacometti's sculpture *Palace at 4 A.M.* Maxwell devotes two pages to the work, describing what "the palace" looks like—its beams, pediment, and tower—and what it contains—a flying creature with a monkey-wrench head, a backbone, and a female figure. Then Maxwell quotes Giacometti's account of how the sculpture came into being. Giacometti relates the work to a love affair in which he and a woman "used to construct a fantastic palace at night, . . . a very fragile palace of matchsticks," continually subject to collapse and renewal. Giacometti tells us, too, that the work's apparent statue of a woman is his mother, as he remembers her from an early memory: "The mystery of her long black dress troubled me; it seemed to me like a part of her body, and aroused in me a feeling of fear and confusion."[35]

Maxwell includes the long description of the sculpture partially because it reminds him of the house frame on which he used to play. We know that when Maxwell walked on this house frame, he had "the agreeable feeling, as I went from one room to the next by walking through the wall instead of a doorway, or looked up and saw blue sky through the rafters, that I had found a way to get around the way things were."[36] In some ways, Maxwell's book permits him to do the same by allowing him to re-create the past. But that's not all the sculpture means to Maxwell, because it relates so obviously to his grief about his mother and to his feelings about the new house and his friendship with Cletus, just as Giacometti's account relates to the very issue of creativity and ruin that is at the center of *So Long, See You Tomorrow,* to matters of imagination and the lost past, construction and reconstruction.

I don't want to suggest that the novella had its origins in Giacometti's work, but that the work does seem to contain the whole of the novella in it, in much the way that we see the part fitting to the whole and the whole fitting to the part in a short story. Even the self-consciousness that Nemerov finds in so many novellas is present in the Giacometti sculpture, or at least in Maxwell's experience of that sculpture, since he presents the "terribly strange and spare" work to us along with the "no stranger" account of its creation.[37]

In the end, perhaps what makes the novella a separate and special form is simply that there are so many more parts to fit to the whole, which may be why the result can seem like a tour de force. All those connections made. So much of the world assembled for us, and in such a small space. The big genie in the little bottle. Where he—at least sometimes—belongs.

Border Guard
FABULISM IN STUART DYBEK'S "HOT ICE"

NOTHING OCCASIONED my twin sister's impromptu performances. We might be out for a walk at Rocky Woods, or having our best friend, Bertha, over for ice cream sandwiches, or hanging out with our younger siblings in the TV room, when Laura would begin: "My most embarrassing moment of first grade was when Jeremy Hart walked in on me in the bathroom. My most embarrassing moment of second grade was when I went to the blackboard to finish an equation, only my skirt was tucked into my tights." Apropos of nothing, it came, the Most Embarrassing Moments List, which grew one sentence longer every year. Seventh grade. Eighth grade. Each line delivered with no inflection whatsoever. Laura was the Steven Wright of most embarrassing moments. Steven Wright, as you may know, is a stand-up comic whose toneless delivery and weird pauses account for half of his humor. "I've got a map of the United States," he says flatly, then waits a beat. Waits a beat. "It's life-size." My sister is well educated, and the Most Embarrassing Moments List encompassed high school, college, and eventually the years in which she pursued graduate degrees in urban planning and architecture. "What's with the emphasizing the failure?" my father must have said one too many times, and the Most Embarrassing Moments List fell out of Laura's repertoire. And entered mine, since I am still in school, only not as a student but as a teacher.

And thus: my Most Embarrassing Teaching Moment.

It is a spring day in Massachusetts. Actually, the first really nice day in a long time, so my composition students have hoisted open the warped windows of our classroom, for the breeze and for the sense (one can't help but suspect) that even though we are reading the first terrible chapter of John Hersey's *Hiroshima*—this is the chapter in which Hersey describes what six people were doing at the moment the bomb dropped—we can't possibly live in a world where such things happen. Nuclear weapons and early dogwoods and the happy shouts of Frisbee players in the distance? Impossible. But, of course, this is Hersey's very point, and since the point is so important (*don't forget, don't forget*)—and since Hersey was *my* writing teacher in college—I'm particularly impassioned. Wanting to do justice to the work and all. I've got *Hiroshima* open in my hands, and I'm reading, with as much fervor as I allow myself in public, the chapter's closing paragraph. As I do, a gust of wind comes through the window, toppling my large handbag and sending half a dozen super tampons rolling like Lincoln Logs into the center of the classroom. "And so," I say, standing, as if absent-mindedly, "'There in the tin factory, in the first moment of the atomic age'"—I bend and start retrieving my wayward "feminine hygiene" products—"'a human being was crushed by books.'"[1]

Exposure, of course, is at the center of my sister's embarrassing moments. And mine. Exposure of the body. But worse, of course, is exposure of the mind. I tell the tampon story as a joke. But the next most embarrassing moment on my list—and I'll stop after two, having learned from my father that it is more fun to list than listen to these moments—occurred when I was working at Emerson College, in a year when I was teaching five different classes in one semester, running from Tufts University to Emerson to the Museum School and feeling like a life which involved paper grading and finding a parking space in Boston—not once but several times a day—was a life that was simply too full for me. All of which is to say that when it came to class preparation, sometimes I'd just wing it. Particularly in my night class in contemporary American fiction, as my graduate students were so bright, they almost always carried the discussion for me. I'd put Stuart Dybek's "Hot Ice," one of my favorite stories, on the syllabus. When the night of the class arrived, though I'd scheduled an hour for discussion, I didn't bring any notes. The story was fabulous and complicated. I knew we'd come up with something. Only we didn't. The class was uncharacteristically silent when I threw out some vague opening question like, "What do you think of this?" I couldn't come up with anything more pointed to focus the conversation. Maybe because I was so in love with the story. "The more you love a story," writes Allan Gurganus of John Cheever's "Goodbye, My Brother," "the stronger is your impulse to illuminate its virtues by simply quoting from the thing."[2] I tried to stumble through class on enthusiasm. Isn't that a great opening? Isn't that a great line? Don't you love that thing about Eddie collecting his favorite urban windows? Lots of praise, but—as book blurbs prove—the language of admiration can seem woefully hollow, not nearly as informed as critical language. The class was a true disaster, and I have a vague memory of talking faster and faster—as I do when I get nervous—finally eliding everything together into a mishmash of half-completed sentences and thoughts till it all ended with something like a "magicalwildimargeryanddon'tyou thinkitshotinhereandweallneedabreak?"

At the time, the story defeated me in another way, too. Imitation— we are told—is the sincerest form of flattery, and I had—I still have— an unfinished story that was my attempt to do what Dybek does in "Hot Ice." But, of course, I didn't succeed, because I'd never figured out what "it" was. I had my feelings about the story but no ability to articulate those feelings, certainly not to convey their intensity.

On the one hand, I know why I failed so badly all those years ago, and on the other hand, I'm completely puzzled by that failure, as there is so much to talk about in "Hot Ice." In his essay "Reading," Richard Ford describes his early uncertainty about how to teach literature despite his awareness of how to read it and how to write about it. "Literature," Ford remembers his graduate school self thinking,

> was pretty and good. It had mystery, denseness, authority, connectedness, closure, resolution, perception, variety, magnitude— *value,* in other words, in the way Sartre meant when he wrote, "The work of art is a value because it is an appeal." Literature appealed to me.
>
> But I had no idea how to teach its appealing qualities, how to find and impart the origins of what I felt.

In the end, Ford turned to his professor—a man named Howard Babb—for advice. Together they considered a Sherwood Anderson story. "What do you think," Babb asked, "is the most interesting formal feature of this story?" Ford admitted he didn't know what a formal feature was. Babb stood and put a list on the chalkboard.

"Character, Point of View, Narrative Structure, Imagistic Pattern, Symbol, Diction, Theme." Then he explained that in all the stories he had read, one formal feature stood out as a "conspicuous source of interest"—in *The Great Gatsby*, for instance, it was point of view—and he used that most striking formal feature as a way into the story.

If anything, "Hot Ice" has too many interesting formal features. There's the point of view, third person, but steadily in Eddie Kapusta's mind, until the final section of the story, when we view things through another character's, Big Antek's, mind . . . or through a limited omniscient narrator. Arguably, it could be either, and how one reads the point of view in the story's final section accounts for how one understands the closing, as well as the story's overall preoccupation with legends and belief. There's the story's overall narrative structure, broken into five different sections and within each section alternating between past and present, so that the story's structure reinforces much of the story's content, with its focus on the characters' relationship to the near and distant past. Even if one moves beyond Ford's teacher's list, there's plenty to talk about—the import of setting, how time is established, the story's fabulist feel. How, how, how, given all this, could one stumble the way I did years ago? Well, like Ford, I probably didn't know enough about teaching. But there's something else.

In his short short story "Fiction," Dybek writes of a man who wants to pay tribute to his lover by telling her a story that will be like "a tune impossible to find on a piano, an elusive melody that resides, perhaps, in the space between the keys where there once seemed to be only silence."[3] This story, the man thinks, might not even concern itself with sounds and silences but start with a smell. In the end, the man wants a story that will go where language can't take him.

In a 1998 conversation with Don Lee, the editor of *Ploughshares*, Dybek makes it clear he longs after the same thing:

> When I first started writing, I thought it would be about *saying* something. I don't think that way now. I think of writing as *making* something. What's come to fascinate me more and more is trying to use language the way that the mediums of other arts—music in particular—are used, so that they lead you to nonverbal places. I don't know if it's a paradox or just foggy thinking to believe language can do the same thing, that language can in some way or another lead you to something unsayable.[4]

In the end, there *is* something inexpressible about "Hot Ice," and that is part of its magic.

FOR THOSE who haven't read it, a quick summary. "Hot Ice" is a story about three young men—Eddie Kapusta and his friends, the brothers Manny and Pancho Santora—all of whom live in a decaying South Side Chicago neighborhood populated by working class Poles, Hispanics, and Czechs and dotted with bars, cathedrals, and rubble. The young people of "Hot Ice" are lost but united, nonetheless, by being outsiders together. A different Dybek story, "Blight," opens with the line, "During those years between Korea and Vietnam, when rock and roll was being perfected, our neighborhood was proclaimed an Official Blight Area."[5] "Hot Ice" clearly takes place in the same neighborhood, only it occurs during Vietnam.

"Hot Ice" starts in the past, with a legend about a local girl, a virgin, who goes rowing with some boys. Rather than succumb to the boys' sexual advances, the girl jumps into a lake and drowns. Finding her, the girl's father carries her—via streetcar—to an icehouse, where "crazy with grief he sealed her in ice."[6]

This legend frames the entire story, which moves from an initial section (subtitled "Saints"), in which the boys consider the legend and an elaboration of it by Big Antek, a neighborhood drunk, to sections subtitled (respectively) "Amnesia," "Grief," "Nostalgia," and "Legends." The later sections take place after Pancho has been incarcerated; during those sections Eddie and Manny wander the neighborhood, often ending up on a nameless street bordering the county prison. At first they yell encouraging words at the prison wall. Later, when Pancho is apparently gone, dead or permanently missing from their world, Manny (with Eddie quiet but in tow) spends two nights yelling curses at the inmates. Eventually the story moves from Pancho's Lent-time disappearance, up through Holy Week, where a final drug-addled walk leaves the boys at the icehouse. With Antek as guide, the boys break in and free the ice-encased virgin before a city wrecking ball demolishes the building that holds her.

UNUSUAL AS it is, this plot description leaves out most of what is special about "Hot Ice." Partially because we're not dealing with a traditional plot with a rising and falling action—not that (whatever the writing books say) that's all that common. "What I love about the short story," Dybek says, "is that you can jump into it where it's already geared up at a high level, start out already in third gear and kick it into forth and fifth. . . . What I like is rising, rising, rising action."[7]

Certainly "Hot Ice" bears out Dybek's affection for rising action. But I never particularly noticed this feature of "Hot Ice" till I read Dybek's comment. What I notice—what I love—about this story is its marvelous invention. Funny, complex, and moving, "Hot Ice" is ultimately a tribute to imagination itself. I find the story—on a line by line level and taken as a whole—completely surprising. Not in the "Oh ho! I never knew that would happen" way, but because I never know where the story, or, indeed, any given sentence, is going. The terms of "Hot Ice" are constantly being revealed and then rerevealed to me. I don't have a sense of narrative tension about what will happen next exactly. Not in the way that in a different sort of tale I'd wonder, say, if adultery will or will not take place and what the emotional results will or will not be for the lovers and the cuckolded parties. Rather I feel a narrative tension about the art itself: what sort of story is it that I'm reading? I have a sense of an impressionist painting. As a reader, I'm a viewer, standing inches away from the Monet—pretty dots and dabs of color that click into an image only when I pull back from the painting. Oh, yes, haystacks. I take pleasure in unity, in finding out how things connect. And then there's the thrill of the story's wildness. There's a particularly interesting brand of fabulism here. It starts with the "weirdness" for which the boys have a fondness, includes hyperbole and juxtapositions that border on the fantastic, crosses into the extraordinary perceptions of lyricism, and ends in "actual" magic. All of which is made more complex by the issues of faith and belief that are so much a part of this story. And by the vanished, vaguely recalled past—"It was hard to believe there ever were streetcars," Eddie thinks[8]—which contributes to the unreality of the characters' world.

IN "AMNESIA," the second section of "Hot Ice," the past is literally crumbling around the boys. They walk through a weedy landscape of gutted factories and boarded-up buildings with wrecking balls poised to knock away more of the past. The first man, says a Nandi child in Beryl Markham's *West with the Night*, "worried very much because he could not remember yesterday and so he could not imagine tomorrow."[9] And so it is with Eddie, Pancho, and Manny. Because they can't fully recall the past, because they can't comfortably relate to it even though they value it, they are somehow insufficiently real themselves.

The mere fact that the story starts in the past, with the legend of the drowned girl, is crucial. The legend itself should be horrible. But it's not. It's oddly beautiful, part of Eddie's tribute to a world he doesn't quite remember, not a world of "order exactly but rhythms."[10] The exact story of what happened to the drowned girl is unknown. "It was necessary," the narrative tells us, "for each person to imagine it for himself."[11] And in Eddie's imagination, the moment of near violation is erotic, lyrical.

> One of them stroked her hair, gently undid her bun, and as her hair fell cascading over her shoulders surprising them all, the other reached too suddenly for the buttons on her blouse; she tore away so hard the boat rocked violently, her slip and bra split, breasts sprung loose, she dove.[12]

As Dybek says of writing itself, "Imagination is the ultimate defense."[13] Here, imagination has the effect of transforming the legend into something useful, something Eddie can value, though he admits, "He didn't want to wonder what she remembered as she held her last breath underwater."[14] Instead Eddie skips to the next poetic moment of the tragedy—the father racing his daughter to the icehouse—only to be interrupted in his memory by dialogue. "'I believe it up to the part about the streetcar,' Manny Santoro said that summer when they told each other such stories, talking often about things Manny called *weirdness* while pitching quarters in front of Buddy's Bar. 'I don't believe he hijacked no streetcar, man.'"[15] This line, coming seven paragraphs into "Hot Ice," does several things at once. First, it reminds us of an arguably funny aspect of the story. There's something comical about the workaday streetcar being combined with the legend of the saint, and Manny is highlighting this for us. He's also bringing up the whole issue of belief, as he brings the legend into the present, slightly recasting it with his slang ("he hijacked no streetcar, man"). The line also gives us the "now" of the story. Until this moment, we've had a legend, and a character (Eddie) who has heard the legend and thought about it, but we're not aware that Eddie is anywhere physically, that he's placed in space or time.

Manny's words let us know where Eddie is—he's in front of Buddy's Bar, the bar to which the story will return, again and again—and what time it is—it's "that summer when they told each other such stories."

We stay in the "now" for two brief paragraphs, and then the story goes into summary for four paragraphs, giving us other versions of this same conversation about the virgin and faith, letting us know a bit about the brothers, their relationship, and their beliefs. Pancho "believes in everything," ghosts, astrology, saints. Pancho's brother, Manny, is the skeptic. Everything is bullshit to him. As for Eddie, he's an agnostic. He shrugs when asked about his beliefs, "Not that he didn't have any ideas exactly, or that he didn't care. That shrug *was* what Kapusta believed."[16]

When we return to the "now" of the story, we are returned to the discussion of the virgin, with Pancho saying, "I believe she worked miracles right in this neighborhood, man." This discussion runs to the end of the "Saints" section of the story, with one digression into Big Antek's anecdote about the frozen virgin. The conversation is entirely particular, but it stands for all the other conversations the boys have had about this issue during the summer of discussing "weirdness."

Normally writers are told to be careful about grounding readers in the here and now, establishing things, before wandering off into the past or a digression. Then, writers are reminded to pull the reader back, before too long, to the "now" of the story, to keep the reader *located*. Dybek's strategy, however, works for a number of reasons. First, form is mimicking content. Past then present, because past is more present than present for the boys. ("There was no present—everything either rubbled past or promised future.")[17] Second, detail. Part of the reason writing teachers says flashback is a no-no is because writing students tend to use *abstract* summary when they leave the present. But if you do the past as "sensual summary" (Dybek's term), if the past is as detailed as the present—and it certainly is in Dybek—then why not make use of what Dybek calls "one of the great gifts of your art form: an ability to travel forward and backward in time"?[18]

BECAUSE HE writes about Chicago and urban reality, some reviewers have compared Dybek with the hardcore realists of the Chicago tradition, writers like Saul Bellow, James T. Farrell, and Nelson Algren. Certainly an appreciation of the curious or absurd detail isn't outside the realistic tradition. Or the realm of "Hot Ice." Army tanks go down inner city streets; leaves rustle by the boys' shoes, though there are no trees in sight; a war hero shoots his wife in the face while she is ironing. Weirdness, as Eddie, Manny, and Pancho might say. And there's the weirdness of putting a boy like Pancho—a boy, who in his brother's eyes, has a vocation, only not to be a priest, but an altar boy—in prison. The absurdity of fathers sending their sons to war, when, if they come back at all, they come back damaged as Big Antek, the Korean War vet and butcher. But, of course, Dybek's work isn't in the realistic tradition. The "magic" extends well past the curious, and it isn't present just in "Hot Ice" but in much of Dybek's fiction, as in a story called "Nighthawks," where a kiss travels around the city à la the nose in Nikolai Gogol's "The Nose." Or as in "I Never Told This to Anyone," where a tiny bride and groom, their shoes "covered with frosting as if they'd walked through snow," make nightly visits to a boy's bedroom.[19]

Dybek's impulse to combine the real and the fantastic or pseudofantastic has its origins in music. Or at least this is the story he tells. As a writer, Dybek hadn't quite found his voice till he started listening to Bela Bartok and Zoltan Kodály, composers who, Dybek explains, "were part of a movement which tried to infuse postmodern music, mainly French impressionist music, with folk elements from their own culture." To do this, they explored the Hungarian countryside, recording Gypsy music on early recording devices. What they found was "true primitive stuff based on bagpipe riffs, and strange model chords," all of which they tried to incorporate into their own work. The first time Dybek heard a Kodály recording, he says, "I sat down and wrote a story . . . that I had never even thought about writing. It was literally almost like falling into a trance. I think what happened was the same thing that happens in a fifth grade classroom when the teacher brings in Ravel's *Bolero,* and says to the kids, 'Now, kids, today we're going to listen to Ravel's *Bolero,* and you write whatever comes into your mind.' . . . and everybody is writing, 'I see camels going across the desert. They're dancing at the oasis.' [Kodály's] music just brought up all these images, but the images it brought up happened to be these Eastern European images, which, on some levels, I guess I had grown up with, but had never been able to harness or tap into."[20]

Later, Dybek found literary precedents for what he was doing in his writing. His reading, which had previously tended to American realists like Hemingway and Sherwood Anderson, started to focus on Eastern European and Hispanic writers, the so-called magical realists.

At times, in "Hot Ice," Dybek's "magic" *does* seem apiece with the surprises of Kafka and Gabriel García Márquez. A frozen girl keeps a man, locked in a meat locker, from freezing to death. A dead girl radiates golden beams from a block of ice. Elsewhere, even though belief is constantly at stake in "Hot Ice," the "magic" of the work is so linked with the real that it seems more like an extension of the real. Eddie, in listing who used to be imprisoned in the county jail, remembers, "Billy Gomes, who set the housing project on fire every time his sister Gina got gangbanged."[21] This might be literally true, but it has the sense of a playful (if terrible) exaggeration. At times, Dybek's "magic" *is* a joke, something the imagination can do, so why not let the imagination do it? "He got," says Manny of his fanatical brother, with his many crosses, hanging around his neck and tattooed on his wrist, "a cross-shaped dick." "Only when I got a hard-on, man," Pancho says.[22]

Not true magic here, but a fantastic image, nonetheless, one that the brothers reach by the power of their imagination. And exaggeration. We see this again in the description of Big Antek, the butcher who "drunkenly kept hacking off pieces of his hands, and finally quit completely to become a full-time alky."[23] Or when Pancho talks about all the people he thinks are saints—like the superdevout Mrs. Carillo, who "prayed all day and they thought she was still praying at night, and she was kneeling there dead."[24] Again, a fantastic, terrible, but funny image. Should we trust it? Well, maybe not, but, of course, we don't need to *believe* the image to take pleasure in it.

Hyperbole, often a sort of speculative hyperbole that is only half serious, is a staple of a certain kind of writing, one that wants to touch on extreme possibilities but not fully engage them, as in the "Grief" section of the story, where the first paragraph lists the rumors, increasingly fantastic but never impossible, about Pancho's disappearance from prison.

Pancho had hung himself in his cell; his throat had been slashed in the showers; he'd killed another inmate and was under heavy sedation in a psycho ward at Kankakee. And there was talk he'd made a deal and was in the army, shipped off to a war he had sworn he'd never fight; that he had turned snitch and had been secretly relocated with a new identity; or that he had become a trustee and had simply walked away while mowing the grass in front of the courthouse, escaped maybe to Mexico, or maybe just across town to the North Side around Diversey where, if one made the rounds of the leather bars, they might see someone with Pancho's altar-boy eyes staring out from the makeup of a girl.

Some saw him late at night like a ghost haunting the neighborhood, collar up, in the back of the church lighting a vigil candle; or veiled in a black mantilla, speeding past, face floating by on a greasy El window.[25]

In the end, the fabulist feel to these paragraphs isn't about magic or the impossible. They're about putting things together—a young man and a black mantilla, Pancho and leather bars—that don't normally belong together. Even the juxtaposition of language, Spanish and English, creates this effect for Eddie, who hears something lovely—"cooing and the whistling rush of . . . wings" in *juilota,* Manny's word for pigeon.[26]

BUT, OF course, hyperbole and peculiar juxtapositions don't account for all of the "magic" of "Hot Ice." There are also lyrical moments where perceptions intensify *into* the extraordinary, as in "Grief," the third section of "Hot Ice." Here, the outraged screaming of prisoners, fueled by Manny's sorrow-driven taunts—"We're out here free, man. . . . We're on our way to fuck your wives"—haunts Eddie.[27] He "dreamed they were all being electrocuted, electrocuted slowly, by degrees of their crimes, screaming with each surge of current and flicker of streetlights as if in a hell where electricity had replaced fire."[28] Later, Eddie notices skyscrapers that glow "like luminescent peaks in the misty spring night."[29] Here the "extraordinary" lyrical perceptions are folded into figurative language. But this isn't always the case with the story's lyrical flights, as is most clear when Big Antek remembers being in Buddy's Bar just after the Korean War.

This memory unfolds in the first section of the story, part of a larger anecdote Big Antek tells as evidence of the miracles that the frozen virgin worked, as Pancho claims, "right in this neighborhood."[30] Pancho has heard the anecdote from Antek. But in the course of the boys' discussion about the virgin, the reader hears the anecdote as if through Antek's point of view. Not that Antek jumps out of nowhere and starts narrating his own tale, but the third person narrator segues from the *fact* that Antek told his story to *what* he told and then to Antek's actual experience in two sentences. As follows:

> Big Antek had told Pancho about working on Kedzie Avenue when it was still mostly people from the old country and he had found a job at a Czech meat market with sawdust on the floor and skinned rabbits in the window. He wasn't there a week when he got so drunk he passed out in the freezer and when he woke the door was locked and everyone was gone.[31]

After this, the story of Antek's weekend in the meat locker begins in Antek's point of view: "It was Saturday and he knew . . ." This shift preps us for the surprising move into Antek's point of view in the final pages of "Hot Ice." For now, we have the tale of how Antek, unable to escape and knowing he'll die before the weekend is out, makes his way back to a cooler, where he finds the virgin, frozen in ice. Her hair, we learn, is "not just blonde but radiating gold like a candle flame behind a window in winter."[32] The sight of the girl calms the panicking Antek and keeps him alive, somehow, till Monday morning. A miracle. "True" magic. But almost as miraculous is the recollection that comes to Big Antek, just before he sees the frozen virgin. Her cooler reminds him of a similar cooler, one that Antek saw his first summer back in Chicago after Korea. This was at Buddy's lounge—the very lounge where we first see Eddie, Pancho, and Manny hanging out—a place located across the street "from a victory garden where a plaque erroneously listed [Antek's] name among the parish war dead." Years ago, while reaching into Buddy's cooler for a beer, Antek looked out through the tavern door and thought that the girls on the street looked like blondes in a movie, "a movie full of girls blurred in brightness, slightly overexposed blondes, a movie he could step into any time he chose now that he was home; but right at this moment he was taking his time, stretching it out until it encompassed his entire life, the cold bottles bobbing away from his fingertips, clunking against the ice, until finally he grabbed one, hauled it up dripping, wondering what he'd grabbed—

a Monarch or Yusay Pilsner or Fox Head 400—then popped the cork in the opener on the side of the cooler, the foam rising as he tilted his head back and let it pour down his throat, privately celebrating being alive." Back in the meat locker, Antek remembers the earlier moment as "what drinking had once been about," and he concludes, "It was a good thing to be remembering now when he was dying with nothing else to do about it. He had the funny idea of climbing inside the cooler and going to sleep to continue the memory like a dream."[33]

THE INTENSITY here *is* out of the ordinary—it's extraordinary—though not, of course, beyond the "real." Here's Dybek—talking about writing in general, though he might very well be explaining this paragraph:

> What I'm always looking for is some door in the story that opens on another world. A doorway like that can be religious experience; in fact, that's probably the first such doorway I was aware of. When I grew up on the southwest side, the two biggest landmarks on most every corner were a church or a tavern. I would be walking down, let's say 25th street, which would represent ordinary reality. Ordinary reality would be made up by bread trucks delivering bread, people going to work, kids playing on the sidewalk, women hanging wash and so on. But by just stepping through either one of those doorways, the tavern or the church, it seemed to me that you entered a different world. In the tavern you entered a world that moved to a different time. The time it moved to was whatever song was on the jukebox. There was the smell of alcohol. People told stories and behaved in ways they would never behave on the street. The church was the same thing. By just entering its doors you just seemed to enter the medieval ages. There was the smell of incense, and there were statues of saints and martyrs in grotesquely tortured positions. What I look for as a writer in stories are those doorways in which somebody leaves ordinary reality and enters some kind of extraordinary reality.[34]

In Dybek's first short story collection, *Childhood and Other Neighborhoods,* childhood itself seemed like a doorway to another world. In

"Hot Ice," the borders between different worlds proliferate. Literally—borders, like viaducts, are permanent; everything else in the neighborhood is subject to change—and metaphorically. Past and present. Secular and profane. World of the street and world of the tavern or the church. The living and the dead. Even the nameless street that edges the prison, more of a shadow than an actual street, serves as a literal and metaphorical border between worlds. Ethnicity, too, is arguably a doorway to another world. So, of course, are drugs, particularly in the fourth section of "Hot Ice," the section called "Nostalgia," where the boys are tripping as they reenact a ritual of their earlier childhood by trying to visit seven different churches on Good Friday.

Whenever Eddie and Manny go for walks in this story, they are high. At least, they're always sharing a joint. But in "Nostalgia," the drugs are more serious—speed and Quaaludes—and the sense of disorientation is more complete, with day melding into night, and nights running together, so the characters say more than once, "It's like one long night."[35] And yet time becomes more concrete in this fourth section of the story. One could argue that the boys—jittery with speed—are more messed up than they've ever been, but the form of the story suggests otherwise, indicating that the boys are coming to something important, that they are getting closer and closer to incorporating the past successfully into the present. As Robert Wilder, a writer and instructor at Santa Fe College Prep, observes, "What needs to be unified in the ending [of 'Hot Ice'] is the relationship between past and present."[36] At story's end, the boys haven't forgotten Pancho, or their childhood memories (of fishing for smelt, of eating bismarks), or the legendary past. If anything they're better able to access the past when they're on speed than they have been earlier. Or at least Manny, the endless skeptic, is better able to speak of the past. This, of course, isn't the same as reconciling with the past, but it does represent the possibility of holding the past and present—as Eddie holds his favorite windows in order to have a sense of the entire city—together in the mind. What's more, the narrative itself is able to view the boys' histories without flashback or summary. We learn about the past, because it is *part* of the present, as dialogue. Manny *tells* about fishing for smelt, a memory in which the borders between the world of water creatures and land creatures, between animals and man, seems to dissolve. Manny's uncle talked to the fish. Manny himself dived into the water and imagined staying there and shedding memory, though, presumably, the most painful memories of his life—those concerning what happens to Pancho—are all before him.

In the first two sections of "Hot Ice," time is entirely relative, scenes anchored by phrases like "that was the summer when they told each other such stories" or "that fall when Manny and Eddie circled the county jail." In starting the tale of Pancho's trial for drug possession, the narrator tells us, "That was when Eddie knew Pancho was crazy." In the third and fourth sections of "Hot Ice," time references change. Events are consistently anchored by religious holidays. By Lent, Pancho is gone; around Christmas, Eddie and Manny stop taking their walks around the country jail and Pancho starts refusing all visitors; by Easter, Eddie has heard Manny is spending time alone, muttering that everything is bullshit. The final scenes of the story start on Tuesday of Holy Week and run through Good Friday, ending (more or less) at 3:00 P.M. ("It had been 3:00 P.M.—Christ's dark hour on the cross—inside the churches all day, but now it was turning 3:00 P.M. outside too.")[37] At this moment, as a capper to the wordless connections he has been making with Manny throughout the long night, Eddie observes the church's old, praying women. They weep, they groan. What, Eddie wonders, do they have to be so ashamed of in their postconfession agony? And yet, Eddie realizes that "a common pain of loss seemed to burn at the core of their lives, though [he] had never understood exactly what it was they mourned. Nor how day after day they had sustained the intensity of their grief. He would have given up long ago. In a way he *had* given up, and the ache left behind couldn't be called grief. He had no name for it. He had felt it before Pancho or anyone was lost, almost from the start of memory. If it was grief; it was grief for the living."[38]

And then, having had this epiphany, and still reeling from all the drugs in his system, Eddie leans back in a pew and lets a stained glass angel overhead serve as something like a visual confirmation of the thought he has just had.

The intensity of this realization and the attendant images of the entire "Nostalgia" section of "Hot Ice" put me in mind of the closing paragraph of James Joyce's "The Dead," where the lyricism is transcendental, where one does, in fact, leap out of the body for a perception that is, nonetheless, of the body, of this world. Snow is general over Ireland. The angel above Eddie's head is a "prism for darkness." And darkness itself, night itself, is part of the past, of the private history that Eddie and Manny share.

IMAGINATIVE DETAILS, "weirdness," the curious, hyperbole, strange juxtapositions, lyricism that intensifies perceptions so they transcend the ordinary. All this sets the stage for a leap away from the real. The final section of "Hot Ice" is called "Legends," and it inverts aspects of the first four sections of the story. One good thing, says Dybek of fragmented forms, is that you get "more first lines and last lines for your buck."[39] Which means what, exactly? Well, more resonant statements for one. More intensification of what is happening in the story as a whole.

"It started with ice," the final section begins. "That's how Big Antek sometimes began the story."[40]

A point of view shift. Our third person narrator is now in Big Antek's head, when he's been in Eddie Kapusta's head for the first four sections of the story. But otherwise the opening of the closing section of "Hot Ice" mimics the story's opening pages: "The saint, a virgin, was uncorrupted. . . . That's how Eddie Kapusta heard it."[41] And as Eddie, in that first section, had to imagine the legend of the virgin, had to work out the details for himself, so Antek has to work out the details of the legend for himself. Only now the legend isn't the story of the virgin but the story of Eddie and Manny, who have become part of the legend themselves by breaking into the icehouse to rescue the virgin. This gives us at least one clue as to why point of view has been switched. A legend isn't for the participants of the legend; it's for those who come after, for those who hear the story. And yet, this legend *is* for the participants of the legend, so Antek's point of view merges eventually with that of the boys, but that point of view is now dominated, surprisingly enough, by Manny. Time has changed, too, in this final section. When does it take place? Well, we don't know. We only sense that it is summer, because of the description of the heat and of Eddie and Manny's antics—rubbing ice all over themselves, and so on. In getting a view of Eddie and Manny from the outside, we see, in many ways, how lost they are—"two guys in the prime of life going nowhere," Antek concludes.[42] Eddie and Manny say they're celebrating when they run into Antek on the street, but they never say what they're celebrating: "Maybe one of them had found a job or had just been fired, or graduated, or joined the army instead of waiting around to get drafted. It could be anything. They were always celebrating."[43] This mirrors, to a degree, the uncertainty Eddie has about the nameless boys who take the virgin rowing: they could have been sailors or "neighborhood kids going off to the war."[44] And just as Eddie and Manny are described earlier as missing something they don't even remember, Antek feels that "there were places deep within himself that he couldn't examine, yet where he could feel that something of himself far more essential than fingers was missing."[45]

In the action of the final pages of the story, Antek waits as Manny and Eddie break into the icehouse. Antek can't see the boys, but he imagines what they must be doing. This mimics both Eddie's version of the virgin's story—the imagined truth—and Pancho's version of Antek's story—the "true" story delivered by immersing one point of view within another. As the scene continues, though, point of view grows fuzzy. Are we getting the scene as Antek imagines it? Or the scene itself? We don't know for sure, though the narrative starts to move into material Antek couldn't possibly know—what the boys say in his absence, for instance—and finally into material that Antek presumably *wouldn't* imagine—the boys deciding to "forget" Antek.

Then in the closing paragraph, there is one last startling shift. We are in Manny's point of view as the boys rescue the frozen virgin. Finally, a "true" miracle. Or "real" magic. The virgin exists, and Manny, in freeing her, in pumping an old-fashioned handcar over the railroad tracks to the lake, is doing what he's needed to do all along, to incorporate the past—his childhood memories—with his city and to do what he never could do before: believe. In believing, Manny becomes, along with Eddie, part of the legend himself. When we last see the boys, they are "rowing like a couple of sailors," leaving the reader with a complicated emotion, connected to the eros of the opening images of the virgin, the poetry of Manny's childhood dip in the lake (where memory—briefly, happily—fled him), and the strange beauty of the dilapidated city. And there's more, more than I can hope to list: the joy of the forthcoming release, the darkness of the possibility that if Manny and Eddie are a couple of sailors now, they also might be (like the original boys of the legend) "neighborhood kids off to war." And finally, there's the mystery of how the real becomes the legendary. "Right before your eyes," as magicians say when they're announcing some sleight of hand.

In the end, though, the "real" magic here is that of belief, which is the issue not just of this story but of art. Is it true? Does the virgin exist? Do the boys really free her using an antiquated handcar? *Was* she a saint? Even though belief is at stake in "Hot Ice," these aren't the questions of the story. The questions are really about the border, about the line between this world and that, about the place where things become extraordinary. And what of the border? I think of John Hersey's *Hiroshima*—that sentence about a person being crushed by books in the first moment of the atomic age, that moment when we crossed from one reality into another. "Three things about the border are known," writes James Galvin in his poem "Cartography," "It's real, it doesn't exist, it's on all the black maps."[46] Beyond this, I don't know what there is to say about the border. I'm returned to one of my most embarrassing moments. Exposing my mind, as decidedly empty. But that's a lie, because I do know something. I know the border itself has power and that Dybek—like some puckish patrol officer, too busy checking out the action to arrest people crossing in and out of the country—has harnessed that power for this story.

Stand Back

My younger brother is safely ensconced in middle age, but he remains attached to the torments he devised as a child. At least the ones he devised for me. So it's not uncommon to find his nose two centimeters from my own, his mouth behind it grinning like some demon jack-in-the-box, as he says, "Am I in your space, Derba?" Derba is the family nickname for me. "Am. I. In. Your. Space?"

When I was ten, this was when I'd haul off and slug him. Now that I have the patience of the sages, I say, "Yes, David, you are, and I can see every one of your greasy blackheads." Or something equally complimentary concerning food in his teeth. And sometimes I defend myself. It *is* unpleasant when someone stands too close to you. Nobody likes it. Or that's not really true, since many of us in the United States have suffered a crowded subway or bus without cringing. What's hard to take is observing and interacting with someone who is too close for the social situation. That's when we step back, to try to get a little distance. I have a writer friend who describes certain contemporary fiction as like watching a movie with your nose pressed to the movie screen. I know the kind of stories she means, and their perspective doesn't make me praise the specificity of detail and intimacy of the narrative. They just kind of piss me off. Now, that's a curious reaction, I suppose, anger, and as the authorities in these matters say, "Rather than express that emotion, why not look at it?" The fact is when I'm up too close I don't see. Or what I see doesn't make me feel a connection. It just kind of puts me off.

ONE TIME, I was at a party for John Irving—this was in my graduate school days—when a woman fainted. I remember Irving standing over the woman, calling out, "Stand back everyone. Stand back." Get too close, presumably, and you'll do damage. Irving's was the voice of authority in that moment; when you're the one who decides where people will and will not stand, you have a lot of power. Is there a narrative equivalent to this social situation? If so, contemporary fiction writers have largely abdicated this power, writing, as we so often do, without employing much, if any, narrative distance. What I mean is what you may have already noticed: that many contemporary narratives are written in first person or in a third person that's a virtual stand-in for the first person. The third person narrator has access to a single consciousness and rarely uses his or her status *as narrator* to offer up much that a single consciousness wouldn't provide. Of course, just because this is the default mode of much contemporary American fiction doesn't mean it's wrong. And nothing that I'm going to say here is meant to contradict that fact.

Still, this is a long essay directed to one simple point: your narrator doesn't need to be your protagonist. Or you, for that matter. Distance can, in some cases, for some stories, be a good thing. And even when distance isn't advisable, it can't hurt to consider options for the narrator-character relationship.

Narrative distance, psychic distance, authorial stance . . . all these terms have been used for what I want to look at: the relationship—in space, in time, in attitude, even in levels of reality—between the narrator and his or her characters.

But first let me step back to put the subject of narrative distance in the context of point of view. You'd be hard-pressed to get yourself through any beginning fiction-writing class in this country without being lectured about the possible points of view available to the writer. You'd be told what you'd probably already observed by grade school. Things can be written in the first, second, or third person. By high school, you'd probably have figured out much of the rest of the lesson—which would consist of a few salient points about each person. The first person narrator can be used to tell a story in which the first person narrator is or is not an essential participant. The "you" of the second person can refer to a character or a reader. The third person is the "tricky" point of view, insofar as the third person narrator has to make a decision in terms of what consciousness, or how many consciousnesses, he or she will have access to.

Within the third person, one can have an objective or bird's eye view narrator—this would be akin to a narrator who is essentially a dramatist, with no access to any consciousness and therefore with the obligation of presenting (i.e., dramatizing) the entire story. There aren't many stories written this way, but two examples of such stories are Richard Bausch's "1-900" and John Sayles's "I-80 Nebraska," both of which consist wholly of dialogue. The former, as the title suggests, concerns a worker and a caller to a sex phone line; the latter is a dialogue between truckers on their CB radios.

There's a good reason that few writers avail themselves of the objective point of view: it ignores one of the essential virtues of fiction. As E. M. Forster notes, "People in a novel can be understood completely by the reader, if the novelist wishes; their inner as well as their outer life can be exposed."[1] I can guess at the inner life of my husband, my child, my students, and the man who sells me stamps, but I can only guess based on what they say and what I intuit from their manner and actions. I'll never have direct access to them. They may be dissembling or unable to articulate their own thoughts accurately. They may be well-disguised monsters from the planet Ur. In a sense, then, I know Anna Karenina far better than I do my mother.

Most contemporary writers open at least one consciousness in their fiction. This sort of point of view is sometimes called third person close. Writers can also avail themselves of selected omniscience (access to some but not all consciousnesses) or complete omniscience (access to all consciousnesses, all at once, or in a serial manner). Whether the omniscience is full or in some way limited, the omniscient third person narrator has the freedom to be objective, to make judgments, to comment on his or her characters, and to move about in space and time. If there is a rule for point of view, it is simply this: stick to one point of view. Don't change horses midstream. If we trust a given point of view, it is called reliable. It we don't, it is called unreliable.

That about covers point of view, or covers it as it is commonly discussed, and the discussion touches on but doesn't really cover what I want to consider. Percy Lubbock in his book *The Craft of Fiction* writes, "The whole intricate question of method, in the craft of fiction, I take to be governed by the question of the point of view—the question of the relation in which the narrator stands to the story."[2] Here, he places the emphasis not on which consciousnesses are opened or closed but the question of distance. Of course, the question of distance is intimately related to the question of consciousness, so narrative distance is really a refinement of point of view.

In *The Craft of Fiction,* Lubbock looks at how questions of distance impact a story's structure, specifically how narrative distance determines how much of a story is done in scene (i.e., as drama) and how much as summary. In a concluding chapter, he lays down his theory about storytelling by imagining a range of possibilities with pure narration on one end and pure drama on the other end. In the case of a tale done as pure drama, "the story itself" is forefronted. It is just presented, scene by scene, as it were. The story is limited to "what the eye can see and the ear can hear."[3] In the case of narration, the storyteller—or "minstrel," as Lubbock calls him—is forefronted, and he gives an account of what he knows, a report to which the reader listens.

Most stories, however, don't exist at these extremes but somewhere along the continuum between narration and dramatization. If you start with the minstrel, with a story that is purely narrated, there are steps which you can take toward dramatization, first by using a storyteller who is in the story he or she tells instead of a storyteller who is unrelated to the tale. Once in a tale, the storyteller can move even further in the direction of drama if he or she becomes the subject of the story. In this case, as Lubbock notes, a decision has to be made about where the narrator's consciousness should be. The narrator can offer an account or report, but, says Lubbock, "if the story involves a searching exploration of his own consciousness, an account in his own words, after the fact, is not by any means the best imaginable. Far better it would be to see him while his mind is actually at work in the agitation, whatever it may be, which is to make the book."[4] In such a case, the narrator should be "forestalled," so the reader can essentially see the story for him- or herself. Of course, once you start to do this, you are pushing even further in the direction of dramatization—presenting scenes, showing rather than telling, and so forth.

And what if you start from the extreme of drama? What might a path down the continuum toward narration look like? What, you might ask, if movies and plays were adapted into novels, not the other way around? There are clear advantages to drama—to just presenting the story to the reader and letting the reader interpret what he or she sees and hears, but not all stories can be presented purely scenically. As Lubbock says, "It is out of the question, of course, whenever the main burden of the story lies within some particular consciousness, in the study of a soul, the growth of a character, the changing history of a temperament; there the subject would be needlessly crossed and strangled by dramatization pushed to its limit. It is out of the question, again, wherever the story is too big, too comprehensive, too widely ranging, to be treated scenically, with no opportunity for general and panoramic survey."[5] In moving away from drama and toward narration, one moves toward "pictorial stories," a story that needs some sort of narrator to "gather up his experience, compose a vision of it as it exists in his mind, and *lay* that before the reader."[6] The story needs someone who digests and presents the material, though here we get into a bit of a morass because there are so many possible ways of doing this. And one actually involves drama. That is, a narrator who presents the story dramatically, distributing it among the characters, who then enact it. Still, even this narrator will need, at some point, to step in more directly "to offer the reader a summary of facts, an impression of a train of events, that can only be given as somebody's narration."[7]

A first person narrator can do all this, can summarize and present material, but such a narrator is restricted by the field of his or her own vision. In many cases, Lubbock argues, a third person close narrator is better, for such a narrator has the advantages of first person (a single, open consciousness) along with several other virtues. The third person close narrator can move about in time, being near or far as need be for the good of the story, and can extend the vision of the point of view character. In third person close, as Lubbock explains, "The seeing eye is with somebody in the book, but its vision is reinforced; the picture contains more, becomes richer and fuller, because it is the author's as well as his creature's, both at once. Nobody notices, but in fact, there are now two brains behind that eye; and one of them is the author's, who adopts and shares the *position* of his creature, and at the same time supplements his wit. If you analyse the picture that is now presented, you find that it is not all the work of the personage whose vision the author has adopted. There are touches in it that go beyond any sensation of his, and indicate that someone else is looking over his shoulder—seeing things from the same angle, but seeing more, bringing another mind to bear upon the scene."[8]

We can go further in the direction of narration to the pure minstrel, but here I'd like to stop, for it is this particular third person narrator, the third person narrator capable of making use of his or her status as a third person narrator, that I want to look at. I want to offer my own continuum, between a third person narrator who functions largely as a first person narrator and other possibilities.

Deborah Eisenberg's story "The Girl Who Left Her Sock on the Floor" has a third person narrator who functions as a first person narrator. The narrative sensibility is completely aligned with Francie, the story's protagonist, and when there is movement—from a direct translation of Francie's thought to a description of the physical world— it is a movement that Francie's own brain makes. For instance, here is Francie, a college girl, in a bus, heading home, in the moments just after learning that her mother and (she believes) only parent is dead:

> How could it be true? How could Francie be on the bus now, when she should be at school? The sky hadn't changed since yesterday, the trees and fields out the windows hadn't changed; Francie could imagine her mother just as clearly as she'd ever been able to, so how could it be true?

And two paragraphs later:

> Out the window, snow was draining away from the patched fields of the small farms, the small, failing farms. Rusted machinery glowed against the sky in fragile tangles. Her mother would have been dead while Francie got up and took her shower and worried about being late to breakfast and went to biology and then to German and then dozed through English and then ate lunch and then hid in the dorm instead of playing lacrosse and then quarreled with Jessica about a sock. At some moment in the night her mother had gone from being completely alive to being completely dead.[9]

Perhaps "fragile tangle" isn't a phrase that Francie herself would utter. There's a good reason for keeping this story third person instead of making it first person, but otherwise the narrative voice here is Francie's. The "and then, and then" list suggests the flow of Francie's young mind, how she's adding things up for herself, not how the third person narrator thinks about things.

Compare this to a paragraph from Margaret Atwood's "Wilderness Tips."

> He scratches his belly under the loose shirt he wears; he's been gaining a little too much around the middle. Then he stubs out his cigarette, downs the heel of his Scotch, and hauls himself out of his deck chair. Carefully, he folds the chair and places it inside the boathouse: a wind could come up, the chair could be sent sailing into the lake. He treats the possessions and rituals of Wacousta Lodge with a tenderness, a reverence, that would baffle those who know him only in the city. Despite what some would call his unorthodox business practices, he is in some ways a conservative man; he loves traditions. They are thin on the ground in this country, but he knows one when he sees one, and does it homage. The deck chairs here are like the escutcheons elsewhere.[10]

This paragraph is still third person and still clearly in the consciousness of the protagonist (or the protagonist of this particular paragraph), but there's a bit more distance here. The language—though it conveys the character's thoughts—isn't a transcription of the way the character thinks his thoughts. And though it may be George himself who thinks the sentence that begins "Despite what some would call his unorthodox business practices," it also might be a third person narrator here, willing to comment on her own unscrupulous creation. There's also a tonal difference in these two paragraphs, one that's related to content, to be sure. There's warmth to the Eisenberg paragraphs. We're meant to feel for Francie in her crisis, and we do feel for her. Atwood's paragraph is distinctly more cold. Of course, George is unlikable and Francie is not, but the tone of the paragraphs drives this home. In another writer's hands, George's interest in traditions might seem like a saving grace, something that humanizes him and makes us feel for the many troubles he's had. (Elsewhere in the story, we learn about how George has survived a brutal childhood.) But that's not Atwood's purpose, and as such, she lets her language create a remove (however slight) from her character. We see through George's eyes here, but we're also looking at George (far more than we are at Francie). We don't see Francie looking at the farms out the bus window as much as we look out the bus window with her. With George, we observe him observing things. We don't, for instance, get a direct sight of the lake, but of his movements—and they have a fat cat unpleasantness given the belly scratching, the Scotch, the hauling himself out of the chair—around the lake.

A large number of contemporary writers use narrators who relate to their stories as Atwood and Eisenberg's narrators do. I write this way myself, and there is a logical reason for writing this way. It mimics the way we are in the world. That is, we all see the world through a single consciousness with which we are aligned. For many stories, perhaps most contemporary stories, the use of a close third person is perfectly appropriate, but I write this essay as a pep talk to people (myself included) who want to experiment more with the storyteller mode.

Here is the opening of Angela Carter's "The Courtship of Mr. Lyon":

> Outside her kitchen window, the hedgerow glistened as if the snow possessed a light of its own; when the sky darkened towards evening, an unearthly reflected pallor remained behind upon the winter's landscape, while still the soft flakes floated down. This lovely girl, whose skin possesses that same, inner light so you would have thought she, too, was made all of snow, pauses in her chores in the mean kitchen to look out at the country road. Nothing has passed that way all day; the road is white and unmarked as a spilled bolt of bridal satin.
> "Father said he would be home before nightfall.
> "The snow brought down all the telephone wires; he couldn't have called, even with the best of news.
> "The roads are bad. I hope he'll be safe."[11]

The lovely girl is the point of view character here. It is she who thinks the final three lines about Father's failure to come home, but she is not behind the observations or the language of the first paragraph. A stand-apart narrator characterizes the outside landscape, comments on the girl's appearance, and judges the kitchen as "mean." Much of the story's language—"spilled bolt of bridal satin," "an unearthly reflected pallor"—owes nothing to the young girl's way of speaking or thinking. Those phrases belong to the storyteller, who is a decided presence here. The storyteller is even more of a decided presence in the opening paragraph of Elizabeth Strout's *Amy and Isabelle,* where there's a narrative voice without (initially) allegiance to any specific character's consciousness.

It was terribly hot that summer Mr. Robertson left town, and for a long while the river seemed dead. Just a dead brown snake of a thing lying flat through the center of town, dirty yellow foam collecting at its edge. Strangers driving by on the turnpike rolled up their windows at the gagging, sulfurous smell and wondered how anyone could live with that kind of stench coming from the river and the mill. But the people who lived in Shirley Falls were used to it, and even in the awful heat it was only noticeable when you first woke up; no, they didn't particularly mind the smell.

What people minded that summer was how the sky was never blue, how it seemed instead that a dirty gauze bandage had been wrapped over the town, squeezing out whatever bright sunlight might have filtered down, blocking out whatever it was that gave things their color, and leaving a vague flat quality to hang in the air—this is what got to people that summer, made them uneasy after a while. And there were other things too: Further up the river crops weren't right—pole beans were small, shriveled on the vine, carrots stopped growing when they were no bigger than the fingers of a child; and two UFOs had apparently been sighted in the north of the state. Rumor had it the government had even sent people to investigate.[12]

In a certain way, this opening is familiar to us from movies. It reads like the establishing shot, in which we pan over the landscape. The distance here is spatial—we're getting a panoramic view—and temporal—we're looking back at "that summer." It's also psychological. We're at a remove from any particular character and united with the narrative sensibility, which is more than willing to characterize a group's feelings and physical responses. We know how both strangers and residents of Shirley Falls feel about the smell of the town. We know *the* precise thing that was so hard to take about the hot, dead summer. There's nothing shilly-shallying about this narrator. She's willing to make categorical statements, lumping people all into one group. She's comfortable offering up a truth that isn't "merely" personal. At the same time, these paragraphs aren't at all abstract. They're grounded in concrete detail. We can see, smell, and feel this town.

The opening two paragraphs of Strout's novel have a tremendous sense of authority. And this sense of authority comes from the combination of generalization and specificity made possible through the presence of a storyteller. We speak of such a narrator as being "omniscient" or as having a "God's eye view," but those words sound vaguely patriarchal, like they'd belong to a narrator whose authority we would want to resist. But the language here—the intimacy of the colloquial *terribly* before the word *hot* or the chatty *just* before *dead brown snake*—makes this storyteller seem decidedly, and appealingly, human. Strout's narrative confidence, her assurance, is comforting. It suggests someone's in charge, someone who knows what's what, someone who is willing to make a statement about things, someone who knows how to tell a good story. This is Percy Lubbock's minstrel. Or seer, as he sometimes calls the storyteller.

As Lubbock notes in *The Craft of Fiction,* the good thing about the seer is that he can go away. Once you've established a more distanced narrative voice in your fiction, you can abandon that voice. This is what, dear readers, our Victorian forebearers did. They might have an entirely intrusive narrative presence, but at times they'd let that narrator step away and let the story play out dramatically. When needed, the narrator who condensed, summarized, and judged was suppressed, and the author offered something more like strict drama—a scene, essentially.

IN *AMY and Isabelle,* Amy forms a relationship with her high school teacher—Mr. Robertson, the same Mr. Robertson who leaves town in the first line of the novel. Here's a scene that comes about midway through the book:

Once Amy was in the car with Mr. Robertson, things seemed a little more normal, although it was earlier than usual, since the school day had been shortened. The sun was high and very hot in the white sky. "Am I going to see you this summer?" she blurted out, not long after they left the school parking lot.

Mr. Robertson glanced at her as though mildly surprised. "I certainly hope so," he said.

"Because on Monday, you know, I start my stupid job at the mill."

He nodded, pulling up to a stop sign. "We'll work it out," he said, touching her arm lightly.

She turned her face away, letting the air from the open window move across her neck; she held her hair in a loose fist, the tips of it tapping lightly against the window frame. For the first time she felt on the verge of a quarrel with him. Such a thing had not seemed possible before.[13]

This sounds altogether different from the opening paragraphs of Strout's novel. The narrator-character relationship here is to the Eisenberg side of the Atwood example quoted earlier. The third person narrator is largely effaced and directly reflects the character's thoughts. The language of the narrator is primarily (though not entirely) Amy's. Later in the scene, we learn, "She almost didn't like him" and "Her skin felt oily, not clean." Occasionally, though, a bit of language creeps in that doesn't reflect Amy's way of expressing things. Just after the scene quoted here, we're told that Amy feels a "dismal petulance" after Mr. Robertson says, "We'll work it out." Still, the third person narrator is not judging here, not commenting, not summarizing. And, of course, it's imperative that the narrator not comment, that no voice come through here to read this moment for Amy or for the reader, for part of the tension of the scene comes from Amy's naïveté and our relative lack of uncertainty about how sketchy (as my undergraduate students say) Mr. Robertson—the seducer in this scene—really is.

A NOTE of caution: you can abandon the seer once you've established the seer, but you generally can't work in the other direction. In other words, if you establish a third person voice that is a virtual stand-in for the first person, it often reads as a mistake if you then back up in your story and try to create a more distanced narrative presence. I sometimes think of this whole matter in terms of how I dress to teach my classes. If I show up the first day in a suit, I seem to have some grown-up authority that I don't have if I wear jeans every day to class. It's fine, then, if I relax my dress and bearing as the term goes on. If I dress in jeans all semester and establish an easy, jokey manner with my students, I can't then put on a suit and use a more formal demeanor in the class. It simply doesn't work.

In talking about her own technique, Elizabeth Strout says, "I see it in terms of a camera. I think the storyteller has to know when to come down with camera and when to pull back. The camera can zoom down for close observation—which is automatically more intense for the reader—but then the reader needs a break. You have to imagine what the reader needs. It's sort of like when you write conversation, you say, 'OK this is enough,' partially because the conversation has served its purpose and visually the reader needs a change."[14]

Of course, one has to be careful to move the camera in a smooth way. According to John Gardner in *The Art of Fiction*, one common fiction writing mistake is a "careless shift in psychic distance." Gardner understands psychic distance as "the distance the reader feels between himself and the events of the story." Consider, Gardner says, these five lines:

1. It was winter of the year 1853. A large man stepped out of a doorway.
2. Henry J. Warburton had never much cared for snowstorms.
3. Henry hated snowstorms.
4. God how he hated these damn snowstorms.
5. Snow. Under your collar, down inside your shoes, freezing and plugging up your miserable soul.[15]

The first sentence in the list is told from a great psychic distance, and then the psychic distance decreases with each subsequent sentence. A poor writer might shift abruptly between these various levels of psychic distance, and the result would be a bit like having a movie camera move in, then out, then out some more and in, and so on, all in a jumpy and senseless fashion. The example John Gardner gives of such a mistake is: "Mary Borden hated woodpeckers. Lord, she thought, they'll drive me crazy! The young woman had never known any personally, but Mary knew what she liked."

More mature writers aren't likely to make this sort of mistake on the sentence level. But on a larger scale, we've probably all had the camera pulled too far back for a given moment (done summary when we should have done scene), and we've probably all lingered too long on a close-up shot. Part of what is so extraordinary about Strout's novel is that she *does* sense the reader's needs, that she utilizes her storyteller according to the demands of her story.

I SAID that I meant this essay to be a pep talk for those who wanted to experiment with the storyteller mode, and I hope I've made clear, if indirectly, the reason for considering such experimentation. The mode has a lot of virtues. It allows one to tell a large story, to give a panoramic view (whether that panorama be of a literal, social, or moral landscape). It allows one to summarize, judge, and comment. It affords one tremendous narrative authority. It permits flexibility in narration, since it can be dropped when need be. I don't think it is an accident that contemporary readers still love Victorian novels. We like the big sweep, the big canvas, the big statements ("It was the best of times; it was the worst of times"). We like Dickens, we like Austen. And Trollope and Eliot. We like their books, but we also like *them*, the storyteller selves who crop up in all their books.

So why don't people use the storyteller mode more? A number of reasons, some of which are worth exploring.

First, I think people conflate narrative distance and emotional distance. In his book *Writer's Mind: Crafting Fiction*, Richard Cohen writes, "The prevailing style in contemporary American fiction favors narrative distance: a cool, detached tone, thoughts and feelings that are implied rather than expressed, and flamboyant technical devices that place a gate between the reader and the character. For example, if a love story is narrated as a collage of phone messages, E-mail transcripts, postcards and office memos, it tends to create a sense of distance even though the characters are expressing their emotions candidly and colloquially. As a result, we're more likely to admire the author's cleverness than to feel anything."[16]

As must be clear, I disagree with Cohen's assessment of this sort of writing as the prevailing style in contemporary fiction, and the collage story he's describing sounds like a bird's eye view story, one without a narrator at all, a pure drama. He's alluding initially, though, to a kind of story that favors style over substance. It's one that creates narrative distance largely through tone, by being ironic and presumably less than fully honest when it comes to emotions.

Cohen continues, "There are times when maintaining that kind of detachment works very well, but there are insurmountable limits to what it can reveal about a character. My own personal preference—my keenest desire when I write first-person fiction—is exactly the opposite: to close the distance between reader and character as much as possible—to maximize the illusion that the narrative is within the narrator, while balancing that with the demands of telling the story."

At the end here, Cohen is acknowledging the "demands of telling the story," which are presumably the demands of a pulled back narrator, but he's saying he much prefers the intimate mode—a straightforward first person narrator or, we can assume, a very intimate third person narrator. Intimacy requires proximity. That's the premise here. And it's hard to argue with.

Jerome Stern, in his own handbook on writing, says essentially the same thing. "When writers are self-conscious about themselves as writers they often keep a great distance from their characters, sounding as if they were writing encyclopedia entries instead of stories. Their hesitancy about physical and psychological intimacy can be a barrier to vital fiction. Conversely, a narration that makes readers hear the characters' heavy breathing and smell their emotional anguish diminishes distance. Readers feel so close to the characters that, for those magical moments, they become those characters."[17]

Again, this makes sense. Who wants to be writing stuff that sounds like a reference book? And yet the beginning writers I know offer plenty of heavy breathing. Indeed, they don't think much beyond the immediacy of the body's expressions of feeling. The one truth they're comfortable offering up is the truth of a single individual in the world—after all, they know what it feels like to be a single individual in the world, and they've been taught, all their lives, not to judge, not to point, not to say anything that would hurt someone's feelings, certainly not to view others in categorical terms. I can't think of Jerome Stern's conclusion without thinking of sentences like

He couldn't believe what was happening to him. His heart pounded, and he could feel the sweat trickle down his back.

and

> She sobbed, and he held her. The tears leaked out of his eyes
> and rolled down into his lips. He tasted their salt.

And when I think of sentences like that I am not frightened or sad.
I am irritated, because I'm too close to the character. I want some distance, and in these cases, I want the distance that comes when one
shows what caused an emotion rather than what the expression of
the emotion felt like. True, there's less narrative distance if you place
me right in the fearful or sobbing body. But perhaps counterintu-
itively, if you establish a remove, you convey emotion better by making your reader feel what your character feels. Now, of course, Stern
wasn't thinking about bad writing when he spoke of narrative intimacy, and the sentences I've imagined aren't strong. Stern was probably thinking of something like the tremendous power of Eisenberg's
narrator in "The Girl Who Left Her Sock on the Floor." There narrative closeness does result in true intimacy. Of course, part of this is
due to Eisenberg's skill—her originality and preciseness of expression, her ability to go deeply and truly into her character—but it's
also because she picked the right point of view for her particular
story.

Let's consider another story that benefits from a different decision
about point of view. This is the opening paragraph of Akhil Sharma's
"Surrounded by Sleep":

> One August afternoon, when Ajay was ten years old, his elder
> brother, Aman, dove into a pool and struck his head on the ce-
> ment bottom. For three minutes, he lay there unconscious. Two
> boys continued to swim, kicking and splashing, until finally
> Aman was spotted below them. Water had entered through his
> nose and mouth. It had filled his stomach. His lungs collapsed.
> By the time he was pulled out, he could no longer think, talk,
> chew, or roll over in his sleep.[18]

Now, that paragraph makes me ill it is so sad. But the narrator
is somewhat distant here. He just presents the facts. In a lesser
writer's hand, you can imagine the paragraph reading something
like this:

Aman could still remember the horrible day when it all happened. He and Ajay were just diving into the pool—like they always did on summer days. There was that intense chlorine smell—the smell of blue, Aman thought, even when he wasn't at the pool—and then Ajay was just lying there. "Mom!" Aman screamed, because he knew something was wrong, "Mom!" Then they were all screaming and crying, because something was wrong with Ajay. Tears were just streaming down Aman's face. His mother kept saying, "Oh, my God. Oh, my God." This was his brother, his own Ajay. What would happen now?

Not a completely terrible paragraph, but not one that's nearly as moving as the first paragraph. Of course, you could argue, this is a very special case. The very enormity of what we're dealing with may require distance. Being close might hurt too much. But, in fact, the distance doesn't protect us in Sharma's paragraph. There's spatial, temporal, and psychological distance in the paragraph. The tone is arguably cold, since it fails to express the emotions that obviously accompany the pool tragedy, yet the paragraph is sickeningly sad. Sharma, too, has chosen the right point of view for his story. The distance here is appropriate, because the distance works.

AT THE start of this essay, I said that I sometimes felt annoyed when I was too close to characters, that proximity didn't always equal intimacy as far as I was concerned. I was speaking then as a reader. But I have the same irritated feeling when I'm writing and I have insufficient distance from my material. I'm talking about when I feel too caught up in my story to work with it in any sensible fashion. Then writing is a chore, and my work is colorless and whiny. I feel a sort of despair. *I can't write. I can't write.* What I need is a toehold on the material, a stance that will give me authority, and often this means a voice that is markedly not my own innermost voice—with its preoccupation with loss and illness or whether people like me or whether I've managed to exercise today—but a voice that's truly a creation, a created thing rather than something merely sunk in myself. This is a process issue, of course, but it's one that *can* be solved by a craft decision to stand back.

I don't suppose I'd want to confess all this if it weren't clear that most of my students feel the same way and that they feel this most strongly when there's another collapsing of distance—between author and character. Then it's easy to hate your fiction. On the one hand, our lives are natural material. At least we know our lives pretty well. On the other hand, as much natural affection as we may feel for ourselves, narcissism and self-hate are two sides of the same coin. But I'll leave aside the conundrum of autobiographical material. My concern is the relationship between the narrator and the character. What exactly is going on in that relationship if you're irritated (as writer or reader)? What's not working?

Well, why not take the relationship to a marriage counselor to find out? We can put the narrator on the chair, the character on the sofa, and the two can talk about how much they piss each other off, how he never does that and she's always haranguing him, and they don't have a relationship at all but a sham of a relationship because they just don't click, they can't connect. Sex? Why the last time they had sex was . . . but I'll interrupt them here, so the wise, nonpartisan therapist can muse that they actually seem quite enmeshed with each other.

Protests from the character and narrator. "What? Are you a loon? Haven't you heard what we just said?"

And here's where the therapist can jump in and explain the psychological concept of differentiation. Which is essentially that individuals in a relationship need to be separate to be connected. The opposite of differentiation is emotional fusion. Presumably when you are emotionally fused with your partner, you are in a relationship—you're in a very intense relationship—but it isn't a good one, because you are getting your sense of identity from the other person. That's why you respond with such irritation to a suggestion or request from your partner or you react so negatively to an opposing opinion from your partner. In a healthy relationship, both partners have separate identities and connect because they want the other person, not because they need the other person to maintain a sense of self. In *Passionate Marriage,* David Schnarch explains that emotional fusion isn't love. It's connection without individuality. Jealousy, then, is emotional fusion taken to an extreme. "At its most severe," writes Schnarch, "jealousy illustrates our intolerance for boundaries and separateness from those we love." Schnarch offers O. J. Simpson as an example: "Regardless of his other culpabilities, Simpson was guilty of emotional fusion. You can't get more graphic than putting your hand on your wife's crotch and saying, 'This belongs to me!' That is, unless you kill her because she's leaving you."[19]

WHAT I want to suggest is that there is such a thing as emotionally fused fiction, fiction that isn't working because the narrator and character don't have separate identities. I don't want to argue that stories in which narrator and character are one and the same are problematic—that would be absurd, given the history of modern fiction—but that sometimes, when a story isn't working, the issue *may* be one of emotional fusion. In which case, differentiation—a stand-apart narrator—may make sense. And how do you know if that's the case? Perhaps when you're working on your story and in a rage. "I hate my story." I've said that. I've heard my students say that. Hate your story? On the face of it, that's absurd. Why such extreme emotion? About seven years ago, my sister called me and asked me what I was doing. "Just working on my dumb fucking novel," I said dispiritedly. Not long after, I got another call: "Hi, Ms. Spark, this is the manager at the Harvard Bookstore, and all our copies of *Dumb Fucking Novel* are flying off the shelf. Could you send more?" It was my sister, of course, recognizing what I didn't. That I needed a little distance.

RICK RUSSO, the author of the Pulitzer Prize winning *Empire Falls*, has always opted for omniscience in his novels, and he likes to remind students that "if you're in third person and only going into one character's thoughts, you still have a choice to make. Are you outside a character and looking into the character or are you inside the character and looking out through that character's eyes?" *Through.* Or *at.* And he cautions, "If you trap yourself in a consciousness, if you limit yourself in that way, the very things you cannot see are going to have to be revealed in other ways. You should have a pretty good reason to do it."[20]

A distanced third person narrator gives you considerably more room to deliver information directly. No messing around with trying to convey, for instance, what your point of view narrator looks like by having her look in the mirror or having a character suddenly muse on his entire history with his mother just so the reader will have that necessary information. The third person narrator can just bypass the point of view consciousness and tell the reader what the reader needs to know to understand the story. This means telling, not showing, of course, but that familiar rule, "Show, don't tell," doesn't mean (as so many people think it does) "Dramatize, don't narrate." It means write vividly and concretely, and you can do that whether you're writing scene or summary.

AT TIMES when we write, we don't want to watch the character. We want to *be* the character, and that is a good reason for limiting yourself to one consciousness—for using first person or third person close.

At other times, we avoid the more distanced third person narrator because it seems arrogant, too lofty a perspective for we mere mortals. And that's probably a bad reason for avoidance, or at least a reason to be jollied out of, even though it's a belief that reflects a prevailing tendency in our literary culture, one that encourages expression of one's personal truth but shies from validating general truths. We're hesitant to declare things. We're willing to say, "I think," but not "It is." We're also uneasy about making judgments in public, though, of course, in private we make judgments nonstop. In this context, the failure to take an authorial stance may seem like cowardice, a failure to own one's thoughts. In which case, we should get over it. In his essay about his teacher, Will Strunk, E. B. White writes that Strunk (as person and as writer) "scorned the vague, the tame, the colorless, the irresolute. He felt it was worse to be irresolute than to be wrong. I remember a day in class when he leaned far forward, in his characteristic pose—the pose of a man about to impart a secret—and croaked, 'If you don't know how to pronounce a word, say it loud!'"[21] Omniscience is a form of saying it loud.

BUT THERE'S another reason that we might avoid the distanced third person narrator: because it's contrived. It doesn't, as I noted earlier, represent the way we are in the world in the way that first person or third person close does, and it leads to statements that just aren't so. It does violence to the truth. Back to *Amy and Isabelle* and Shirley Falls: "What people minded that summer was how the sky was never blue, how it seemed instead that a dirty gauze bandage had been wrapped over the town, squeezing out whatever bright sunlight might have filtered down, blocking out whatever it was that gave things their color, and leaving a vague flat quality to hang in the air—this is what got to people that summer." That's a great sentence. I read it and I'm struck by the originality of the bandage image. I know just what Strout means. But did people—did all the people of the town—really mind that, that specific dirty bandage thing? Is that possible? Well, no. Actually, when you come down to it, how could anyone know what a whole town felt or what the strangers passing through that town felt? We're in the realm of literary artifice. And art, where an imaginative construction and a bit of hyperbole access a felt truth. And it works. So why argue with it, and why not allow yourself it? A storyteller voice, a grand narrator in fiction, *does* involve contrivance, but that doesn't matter as it's a contrivance that departs from literal truth to get at felt truth. Omniscience is pretend, but, then, so is fiction. "If it's true we're all trapped in one consciousness," Rick Russo says, "why would it be true that stepping out of that would be unproductive?"[22] Isn't distorting the truth to get at truth the point?

Omniscience, I should make clear, doesn't necessarily imply a grand narrator—the differentiated third person narrator that I've been considering. You could conceivably allow your omniscient narrator an ability to access different consciousnesses, and to move about in time and space, without establishing a defined narrative presence in the fiction. Flaubert—who makes use of omniscience in *Madame Bovary*—was not at all interested in the grand narrator. According to Mario Vargas Llosa, Flaubert "maintained that what we have termed the autonomy or self-sufficiency of a fiction requires the reader to forget that what he's reading is being narrated; he must be under the impression that it is coming to life in the act, as if generated by something in the novel itself."[23] Writers after Flaubert largely followed his lead, but his theory of the "objectivity" or "neutrality" of the writer doesn't invalidate the power of the novels of the nineteenth century or the usefulness of such narrative styles.

Many writers, no matter what point of view they're using, make use of temporal distance in their stories. They look back at the stories they're telling, sometimes by simply using the past tense when they narrate, sometimes because they're clearly narrating events that happened years earlier. In what I've written so far, I've been largely talking about the advantages of the sort of narrative distance that is spatial and psychological, that assumes a narrator who operates in a narrative space that is apart from the story's narrative space. That narrator is distinct from the story's characters, though he has access to one or more of the characters' thoughts. In *Letters to a Young Novelist*, Mario Vargas Llosa also considers point of view in terms of "levels of reality." Which is to say that a narrator and a story may or may not be in the same place when it comes to level of reality. For instance, you could have a story that exists on a fantastic plane, while its narrator exists on a "realistic" plane. Narrative distance would then be established by the narrator's apparent sense of wonder at what happens in his own story, his sense that the fantastic events are out of the ordinary. By way of example, Vargas Llosa offers "The Dinosaur," a one-sentence-long story by Augusto Monterroso:

When he woke up, the dinosaur was still there.[24]

Since dinosaurs don't exist in our world anymore, this story exists on a fantastic plane. If I dream of a dinosaur, a dinosaur shouldn't still be in my bedroom when I wake. Vargas Llosa notes that it is the single word *still* that establishes the narrator's plane of reality. The *still* suggests surprise, indicates that the narrator thinks this is an odd occurrence, that in the "real" world such things don't happen.

But even within a realist plane, one can have different levels of reality—a more objective sense of the world where events and objects and verifiable phenomena predominate or a more subjective world where thoughts, emotions, and dreams predominate. Vargas Llosa concludes that a discussion of narrative distance and "levels of reality" will eventually give way to a discussion of the form of the novel—realistic, fantastic, mythical, religious, action driven, analytical, psychological, and so on. This broadens the discussion past my specific concerns but reminds one that there are yet more options to consider in the narrator-narrative relationship.[25]

THERE'S A *New Yorker* cartoon that hangs on one of my colleagues' doors in the Colby English department. In it, a sheepish, middle-aged man inquires of a librarian, "Are there any books that are still being written for gentle reader?" Oh, how embarrassing, the cartoon suggests, to want to be told such a story. How embarrassing and natural. The urge may relate to the fact that our first storytellers are often our parents, and there's something comforting in not having to work for a story, in having our folks just tell us how it is. They're so large compared to us. They must know what they're talking about.

Of her own work, Elizabeth Strout says, "More and more I'm realizing all I want to do is tell stories and go ahead and *be* a storyteller."

If you feel the same way, or if you just want to try a grand narrative voice as a departure from the more intimate voices you've used for past work, how should you get started? I'll end with two pieces of advice. In his essay "In Defense of Omniscience," Rick Russo writes, "Omniscience is permission to speak and to speak with authority we know we really don't have, about a world that in our century (any century?) is too complex to know."[26] My first piece of advice is take the permission you've been granted. Don't turn around and ask, "Wait. Are you sure I can?" As soon as you do, as soon as you equivocate, you lose the authority the point of view grants. Second piece of advice: Listen to how people tell stories. I don't mean writers, but people you know who are good storytellers. (Or even bad storytellers. There's always something to be learned from what doesn't work.) I'm thinking, of course, of the kind of listening that isn't fully engaged. So I suppose I'm not advocating listening at all—for then you'd fall under the storyteller's spell—but eavesdropping, behaving like the bratty kid at the magic show, the one who wants the magician's power, the one who so loves the illusion that he wants to destroy it . . . by figuring out how it works.

Cheer Up—Why Don't You?

IN THE wake of the September 11th tragedy—911, the emergency already built in—several news venues spoke of the need for consolation in art . . . and elsewhere. I drive a long way, 140 miles round trip, to work. When I come home, the apolitical whirlwind that is a two-year-old keeps me focused on the most mundane of concerns. I process the international scene, more or less, in the car and with the help of NPR. Last fall, two of NPR's reports particularly moved me. In one, broadcaster Susan Stamberg asked musicians to select a piece of music they'd like America to be listening to right now, "right now" being the fall of 2001. Leon Fleischer picked "Ode to Joy" from Beethoven's Ninth Symphony, since the ode is "to the brotherhood of man."[1] Beverly Sills picked the Casta Diva aria from Bellini's *Norma* because "it's peaceful . . . just as peaceful as can be." Others picked "Amazing Grace" or "Autumn in New York" or "Appalachian Spring," citing their interests in things spiritual, or simple, or American without being military.[2]

In explaining why she initiated the *Music for America* series, Susan Stamberg said, "It struck me that we have obligations beyond the daily conveyance of facts and analysis. And I asked myself how I, as a broadcaster, could add something different to the mix we were putting on the air. The answer came quickly and obviously. Especially as I noticed my own reactions, whenever a brief piece of music (we call them 'buttons') ran between our various reports. Those 10 or 20 seconds of music created a resting place."[3]

The other post-9/11 piece that affected me, also by Susan Stamberg, concerned an exhibition of still lifes at the Phillips Collection in Washington, D.C. The show featured French impressionist work, some of which (given all the disarray in air traffic) hadn't arrived on the day of Stamberg's report. And yet, the exhibit, holes and all, kept to its scheduled opening date. As Stamberg spoke, the still peace of the museum crackled through the radio and into my car in mid-Maine. She described the images before her. Fruit, flowers, shoes. "The ordinary things that make up and pleasure our lives," Stamberg said quietly.[4] I had the desire to pull off to the side of the road and weep. Who knows what kept me from embracing the nearest toll taker? No doubt you have some similar tale of your frazzled self in the weeks after the World Trade Center and Pentagon tragedies. And even as I listened, up floated some lines from Alexander Solzhenitsyn's 1970 Nobel Lecture, lines that often drift through my brain, especially when I think my artist friends are claiming just a tad too much for their work, as if all great virtues, spiritual and otherwise, had to belong to artists to account for our lack of a practical income. "Dostoevsky," writes Solzhenitsyn, "once enigmatically let drop the phrase: 'Beauty will save the world.' What does this mean? For a long time I thought it merely a phrase. Was such a thing possible? When in our bloodthirsty history did beauty ever save anyone from anything? Ennobled, elevated, yes; but whom has it saved?"[5] But to be fair, Stamberg wasn't arguing that art was saving lives, just that it was offering beauty and comfort, a respite, an escape perhaps, a way to return to the troubles of our lives when required.

ON THE same day that the Stamberg Phillips Collection report ran— September 20, 2001, to be precise—the *New York Times* printed an article in which several major novelists complained (to my mind) that their work no longer seemed relevant or claimed that their work was relevant despite everything. "Oh, my people," I thought, ashamed, as when a Jewish person confirms some terrible stereotype about stinginess. Wasn't this just a tad narcissistic? Why weren't we right up there with the visual artists and musicians, thinking about art as consolation or as adequate to expressing the emotions of the tragedy? Or was critic Tom Moon correct when he called Miles Davis's "Blue in Green," from the 1959 album *Kind of Blue,* "prayer music for the times when words no longer work?"[6]

THIS FLEETING thought dovetailed with my realization that it could not be business as usual in my introductory fiction-writing classes at

Colby College, where I've taught for many years. My syllabus, in the week after the tragedy, had students reading Joyce Carol Oates's "Where Are You Going, Where Have You Been?" and Tim O'Brien's "The Things They Carried." Wonderful stories. Mainstays in fiction-writing classes, but given how shaky all of us were already feeling, misguided choices for the moment. Oates's story is about a man willing a girl into compliance with her own rape and probable murder; O'Brien's is about a Vietnam tragedy. My writing exercise of the week wasn't any better. I had planned—back in the summer, when I normally organize my classes—for students to spend fifteen minutes in class writing about the most pleasant thing that had happened to them in the previous week. A pleasant experience that they were willing to share with their classmates. In other words, keep your sex lives to yourselves. Then I was going to have the students pass their exercises to the right. A fellow student would have the assignment of going home and introducing conflict into the experience. Typically, when I do this exercise, I add the caveat that despite the autobiographical origins of the pleasant experience, students are now operating in the realm of fiction, so they can "do" whatever they want to their fellow student's experience without feeling they are wishing ill on a classmate. And thus begins one of my standard lectures on conflict in fiction.

Normally, this exercise is a hit, what with students always interested in finding out what their classmates have "done" with their lives and me able to talk, too, about how writers often segue from experience to invention when they create stories. But in the week after September 11, I clearly couldn't use my exercise. Ask students to write about the most pleasant thing that happened to them in the previous week? If they'd had a pleasant experience, it was something that they'd wrested from sorrow, and the last thing I was going to do was ask another student to introduce conflict into that experience. And talk about the importance of conflict? But imagining conflict didn't seem important. What seemed important was to find peace when there was so much conflict. Sorrow and trouble were all too easy. The challenge was happiness.

I didn't articulate any of these thoughts to my colleagues, but many months later, I found an essay by Bill Roorbach, who happened to be teaching his Colby fiction class down the hall from me on September 11. In the essay, Roorbach discusses his teaching experience in light of his sense that the day's events were unsettlingly familiar. Hadn't the Vietnam militants (about whom he'd written in his first novel) believed violence was the way? And why was he so surprised at this sense of familiarity? Hasn't history already taught us that we hurt each other over and over again? Teaching fiction? When we're all so doomed? Why? Roorbach's temporary despair gives way to his knowledge that violence isn't the only human impulse. "Oh, peace, love," he writes in the concluding lines of his essay. "Write about that, kids. This is fiction class, after all."[7]

A RELATED, but by no means identical, concern. Ever since I first began teaching, fifteen years ago, I've had students ask me why the fiction we read is always such a bummer. The first time this happened, I remember being taken aback. I'd made my own anthology for class and simply picked my favorite stories. "There's death in all of them," one student grumbled. *Surely not,* I thought and scanned down the syllabus. Well, OK, there was James Joyce's "The Dead," but that was a great story, and Margaret Atwood's "The Man from Mars," but that was also a great story, and . . . well, the student had a point. "Wait," I remember calling out, "what about this one. Janet Kauffman's 'Places in the World a Woman Could Walk,' a story about a farm woman?"

"That the one that opens with the woman shooting the cows? The one that has *dead* cows in it?" the student said.

"Oh, yeah," I said. "Well, never mind."

I gave up putting my own anthologies of stories together. Maybe my mind was a little too dark.

DITTO THE minds of Daniel Halpern, Sally Arteseros, Katrina Kenison, Charles Baxter, Janet Burroway, Ann Charters, Ron Hansen and Jim Shepard, Bruce Weber, Patricia Hampl . . . I'm thinking of the editors of the various anthologies I've used over the years in my writing classes. "Why aren't there any happy stories?" a student asked me last year. I brought in a taped version of Daniel Menaker's story, "The Treatment," to play for him in the next class. Which he skipped. And maybe it was just as well, because the story was funny—a riot as read by Isaiah Sheffer for NPR's Selected Shorts— but not happy exactly. In fact, it's about a man, frustrated in work and love, who feels he's having a nervous breakdown, a man who gets into a series of comical discussions with his too-Freud-for-Freud psychoanalyst. I asked a writer friend if she could think of any happy authors, and she said, "Why there are plenty, like Lorrie Moore." Lorrie Moore! A wonderful writer, a funny writer, but happy? Certainly not. I'd put her right up there in the clinically depressed pantheon with a lot of my favorites. So who? So what? The anonymous *Publisher's Weekly* reviewer on *Best American Short Stories 2001*: "intellectually stimulating and satisfying but the inclusion of a few lighter selections might have leavened the mix."[8] A fair conclusion? Should we—we fiction writers—lighten up?

"Peace, love. Write about that, kids." OK, OK. But it would help if we had some models for such fiction.

IN LITERATURE, what sort of work consoles and uplifts? Not necessarily happy material. Look at poetry. What a long list of poems there are that directly address the sort of trauma so many people felt in the wake of September 11. Poems that try to make something of our pain (Emily Dickinson, "A day! Help! Help! Another day")[9] or our concern (John Donne, "I am involved in mankind")[10] or our sense about how to persist in the light of sorrow (William Stafford, "Tragedies happen; people get hurt / or die; and you suffer and get old. / Nothing you can do can stop time's unfolding. / You don't ever let go of the thread").[11] Or the pain of loving and losing—Mary Oliver's "In Blackwater Woods."

> To live in this world
> you must be able
> to do three things:
> to love what is mortal;
> to hold it
> against your bones knowing
> your own life depends on it;
> and, when the time comes to let it go,
> to let it go.[12]

Of course, fiction can work like poetry, surging up into transcendental moments that enlarge our vision. And we read fiction, as Howard Norman has written of his boyhood self, immersed in the offerings of his hometown's bookmobile, as much as for what we want to enter into as what we want to flee. The fictional world is its own reward, and true readers don't ask for that world to be a priori cheerful. I once read a *Boston Globe* article on Anne Sexton in which a relative of Sexton's recalls asking Anne to "just cheer up." Oh, boy. The eyes roll. My students ask about happy fiction. On my own, it would never occur to me to ask the question.

And, yet, the inquiry does make me wonder if the narrative impulse, which focuses so on conflict, is inimical to the creation of a so-called happy story, whatever that might be.

WE'RE TAUGHT to think of stories in terms of conflict. In fact, we're taught to think of this as the most basic part of story writing. Janet Burroway states in *Writing Fiction,* the virtual bible on narrative craft,

> Conflict is the first encountered and the fundamental element of fiction, fundamental because in literature only trouble is interesting.
> *Only* trouble is interesting.[13]

"Satan," opines one of my undergraduates, "is the most interesting part of *Paradise Lost.* God sucks."[14]

"Which is why," chimes in his classmate, "you're never assigned *Paradiso.* You're assigned *Inferno.*"[15]

There's drama in trouble—we all know that—and fiction depends on drama.

"Say what you will about it," Charles Baxter writes in *Burning Down the House,* "Hell is story-friendly."[16]

And yet, and yet. All of us peace-loving, left-leaning writerly types. Could we really have chosen such an antagonistic art form? Quoting editor and teacher Mel McKee, Burroway writes that "a story is a war."[17] Scenes in a story are minor skirmishes that precede the epiphany-inducing final battle. That said, after she published the initial editions of *Writing Fiction,* Burroway amended her notion, allowing that the "story as a war" model might be a rather masculine construction of narrative. Might there be another way to think about stories and drama? A model not about conflict but about connection? Why such a "gladiatorial view of fiction," as Ursula LeGuin puts it? Why let "one aspect of existence, conflict, . . . subsume all other aspects"? Granted, the gladiatorial view of narrative is a view that goes back to Aristotle, but it doesn't account for the emotional power of fiction as much as for its forward motion. Conflict makes us turn pages, but it doesn't necessarily explain why we're affected by stories. "Whereas the hierarchical or 'vertical' nature of narrative, the power struggle, has long been acknowledged," writes Burroway, "there also appears in all narrative a 'horizontal' pattern of connection and disconnection between characters that is the main source of its emotional effect."[18]

But even this admission acknowledges the centrality of conflict in fiction. Perhaps it is easier to assent to the power struggle model of fiction when we remind ourselves of the *nature* of conflict in fiction; that is, interior and interpersonal conflict is as interesting as, actually often more interesting than, external conflict. Thus, material that one might not think of as a war—trying to figure out why a person acts as they do, trying to pick the right person to marry, having a child—is nonetheless a conflict.

When I picked Bill Roorbach's brain about this issue of happy fiction, he confessed that the title (and final) story of his book *Big Bend* came about, in part, because he wanted emotional balance in his collection; he wanted to write "something happy." Which he did, but not by avoiding conflict. ("Conflict," he notes, "needn't be negative.")[19] He also wanted to write about an older man, since his collections of stories (all about men and desire) already had a high school boy, a college student, a young man, and several middle-aged men. The published version of "Big Bend" concerns Dennis Hunter, a wealthy, widowed retiree who takes a minimum wage job at a state park. The story focuses on Hunter's crush (entirely reciprocated) on Martha, a middle-aged, married woman. What to do? This is essentially the story's conflict. How to act, given that the woman is married? This dilemma structures the story, and it's a tribute to how much one cares for Hunter that one hopes—whatever one's feelings about extramarital hanky panky—that he will, as one of the cruder men on his work crew suggests, "go for it." The pleasures of Roorbach's story are many, but they include the enjoyment the narrator takes in his work crew buddies, his ability to find something funny or winning in all of them, and his genuine delight in bird-watching Martha: her laugh, the "fatty dimpling" of her thighs, her "capacious heart."[20] "Big Bend" *is* a warm, happy story, but it earns this status by being well aware of class privilege and class deprivations, the pain of loneliness, the difficulty of love, as well as the beauty of the south-western desert and the gift of mutual affection.

IF A happy story isn't a conflictless story, what is a happy story anyway? A story, like Roorbach's, in which characters find each other, in which they seem to appreciate their world? A story with a happy ending? A story about happy people? A light and inconsequential story? Or perhaps . . . well, perhaps there is no such thing as a happy story, perhaps the dramatists are right. We've only got tragedy and comedy. The terrible . . . and the funny.

I ALMOST never compose an essay on the craft of writing without polling my writer friends on the topic at hand. In the flurry of e-mail replies I received in response to my request about happy fiction came these notes.

From fiction writer Eileen Pollack:

> Glad to hear someone is writing about happy fiction—which my mother always urges me to try to write, though I seem incapable of it. The guy I'm going out with pointed out to me that every single story I've ever written had a male character being severely maimed or hit by a fatal disease. This has given me pause.

From historian Amy Godine:

> What a ghastly idea.
> A happy story.
> Yuck.

From a friend who wishes to remain anonymous:

> Ew! You're reminding me—through no fault of your own, mind you—of a hideously annoying interlude that occurred in my most recent MFA workshop, where this dull-witted student droned on about this very issue. . . . Why does everybody write such dreary stories, why can't we choose the light?

So . . . hmm. Let's quickly rule out a few kinds of happy fiction. Dopey happiness. Mere "cheeriness" on the level of plot and character, which seems too simple to do justice to our vision of the truth. Let's rule out fiction that is happy because its agenda is hope rather than truth. I'm not arguing for the fictional equivalent of "solutions" journalism, which is, in the words of Jon Wilson, publisher of *Hope* magazine, "the exploration of social and human problems and challenges in the context of *solutions and possibilities*—as opposed to simply reporting on problems alone."[21] A noble idea, but translate that into fiction, and you've got nonsense. In a lecture, novelist Jean Thompson once recalled how an editor at *Mademoiselle* refused to print her story "until the protagonist's nervous breakdown and total disintegration of personality was turned into 'a positive learning experience' for the reader."[22] That this seems so patently ridiculous, despite the fiction writer's allegiance to the imaginative world, confirms our sense of the wisdom of Flannery O'Connor's words: "The basis of art is truth, both in matter and mode."[23] Hope is nice, but it's also irrelevant.

BUT LET'S leave hope aside. What about happiness itself? Might that not be a worthwhile subject?

"Happy families are all alike," Tolstoy famously says in *Anna Karenina*, but "every unhappy family is unhappy in its own way."

But is this fair? Are happy families all alike? "Oh, no," says novelist Monica Wood. "I think happy families are happy in infinitely varied ways and that happy families are not happy all the time."[24]

All respects to Tolstoy, but doesn't Wood have a point?

Margaret Atwood's widely anthologized story "Happy Endings" addresses this issue by considering the possibility of a happy ending in light (at least initially) of a happy life. Atwood's story opens with these three lines:

John and Mary meet.
What happens next?
If you want a happy ending, try A.

A presumably offers not only a happy ending but a happy story, as follows:

A.
John and Mary fall in love and get married. They both have worthwhile remunerative jobs, which they find stimulating and

challenging. They buy a charming house. Real estate values go up. Eventually, when they can afford live-in help, they have two children, to whom they are devoted. The children turn out well. John and Mary have a stimulating and challenging sex life and worthwhile friends. They go on fun vacations together. They retire. They both have hobbies, which they find stimulating and challenging. Eventually they die. This is the end of the story.[25]

Only this doesn't feel like a story at all. Is it simply because there is no conflict? No. I'd argue that there are no characters here, no characters who resemble people we know, and the writing is bad. (On purpose, given Atwood's larger intent here, which is to refocus readerly attention from *what* happens to *how* and *why* it happens.) Still, if we consider the opening part of Atwood's story out of its ironic context, we have some bad writing. All those adjectives (*charming, stimulating, fun*). Well, whatever do they mean? Different things to different people. This story is boring because it doesn't resemble life. It's full of clichés about happiness, not information about what would make a happy life.

So, yes, Tolstoy is right if this is how you're going to create a happy family. Without the rigor and realism with which one creates an unhappy family, happy families *are* all alike, and they are all boring, or a boring reflection of a certain cultural idea. Take John Cheever's strange little story "A Worm in the Apple." The story is about a "very, very happy" couple, the Crutchmans. Their happiness, or so Cheever's narrator tells us, makes one "suspect a worm in their rosy apple," indeed that "the extraordinary rosiness of the fruit was only meant to conceal the gravity and depth of the infection." The story proceeds through the Crutchmans' happy life, stopping for the presumed communal take on their happiness. Nice house, big windows, two kids. But why not more kids? A nervous breakdown perhaps? And: "Who but someone suffering from a guilt complex would want so much light to pour into their rooms?" The conflict in this story isn't in the happy couple but in viewers so apparently desperate to dish dirt that they'll create ugliness where there is none. We're told that Rachel, the oldest Crutchman child, was "quite aggressive in a mercenary way";[26] after all, every spring she set up a lemonade stand and charged fifteen cents for the beverage.

One looks but doesn't find the worm in the Crutchmans' lives, save for in the eye of the beholder. Cheever's story seems predicated on this joke. And it *is* funny. What with nice gardens serving as evidence of necrophilic tendencies—why else this interest in digging holes?—and so on. But, of course, one can only play a joke out so far. There does seem to be something else going on in Cheever's story. Like: some sarcasm about what a happy life consists of, or what a happy life means to your average resident of Cheever's Shady Hill. And also some general disappointment about the notion of happiness, for why else would one feel so dispirited by the story's final line:

> The touchstone of their euphoria remained potent, and while Larry gave up the fire truck he could still be seen at the communion rail, the fifty-yard line, the 8:03, and the Chamber Music Club, and through the prudence and shrewdness of Helen's broker they got richer and richer and richer and lived happily, happily, happily, happily.[27]

And why four *happily*s? Because we don't believe it, and "we"—not the Crutchmans—are the subject of "The Worm in the Apple." And the story is not truly about a happy couple but about our failure to believe in (or be interested by) such a couple. An unhappy story really, more damning than a story about "mere" jealousy and gossip. But perhaps Cheever, in his satiric purpose, isn't being all that fair to his readers, for it's not that we don't believe in happiness, exactly, but that we don't believe in a life in which nothing bad happens. Every life is full of sorrows. The happy life (or so we imagine) is happy despite sorrows. For even the happy Crutchmans live in a world where they are the haves among have nots, and why doesn't that give them pause? And how do they handle the sorrows of others? The unsuccessful Shady Hillers? Those who have lost loved ones? What happens when the Crutchmans cast their eyes on our country and our world's bloody history?

But does this mean that there's no such thing as a serious look at happiness in fiction? No, I don't think so. There are writers—Laurie Colwin most immediately springs to mind—who seem devoted to writing about happiness, though even Colwin is most satisfying when her work is about how her characters find pleasure in the world, whatever their circumstances, not about characters to whom nothing bad happens. In one of Colwin's early novels, *Happy All the Time*, two basically content men have good jobs and marry the women of their dreams.[28] These women—one a pessimist, one an optimist—are nonetheless well suited to their marriages, with the greatest stress occurring when the optimist wife goes off for a retreat so her marriage won't become too staid, too settled in its happiness. As fun a read as *Happy All the Time* is, and as much as I'd like to be eating all the great food that Colwin's characters always get to eat, the book irritated me. It's funny and beautifully put together, but by novel's end, when one wife gets pregnant, I found myself praying for a miscarriage—not a huge tragedy, but a worm in the apple. Make this character deal with something, please. Barbara Moss, whose work I'll get to in a bit, says of the Southern California world in which she places some of her characters that it lacks what Eden lacks—"variety and vigor"—which is the basic concern of the characters in *Happy All the Time,* that their happiness will lose its vigor, so they need to invent small ways to challenge that happiness. But how real does this particular problem—the pressures of Eden—strike us?

To my mind, Colwin's *Another Marvelous Thing,* published eight years after *Happy All the Time,* is a much more satisfying look at happiness. It's a story, essentially, about a two-year affair between Frank and Billy (Billy's a woman). Though Frank has had minor dalliances before, Billy hasn't, and she happens to genuinely love her husband, Grey, whom she has known since childhood. This is not an obvious setup for a happy book, but the novel—while recognizing Frank and Billy's guilty feelings and Frank's unresolved longings for "more" from Billy, while never sidestepping the complexity of betrayal— chooses to focus on the pleasure of the affair, the nature of extramarital love and passion. A half-full- versus half-empty-glass take on cheating. If my undergraduates were to write such a story, the object of affection would be simply gorgeous with "Stairmaster legs." Colwin never falls into such cultural clichés. Frank loves his mistress, Billy, his schlumpily dressed mistress, whose flaws—no real attention to clothes or the interior of her apartment or food—stand in direct contrast to Frank's wife, Vera, who is so good with domestic details. What's more, Billy (Frank senses from the start) will never "say something loving" to him. Frank loves her nonetheless. On arriving at Billy's brownstone door one Sunday morning, he observes, "Billy was wearing exactly what she had been wearing yesterday and would wear tomorrow. She had not yet brushed her hair, which was mussed on one side and flat on the other, and there was a fleck of toothpaste on her upper lip. His heart expanded like a bellows, and he took her into his arms."[29]

What's more, Billy is, in her humor and confusion, rather winning for the reader as well. After she and Frank first make love, Billy wryly comments, "In bed with Frank and Billy. Chapter one. Frank and Billy have just gone to bed. They have been in bed for who can say how long. Doubtless they will go to bed again, and the funny thing is, they're both married, and to other people! What a situation. How long, they might ask, has this been going on? Who will ask first?"[30]

It is Frank who most often articulates the pleasure of the affair—not the sex per se, but the moments with the loved one. When Frank and Billy are out walking in a park, and deciding (as they often decide) to break up, Colwin's narrative acknowledges,

> They ambled. Actually they were killing time and putting a spin on their last moments all at one. They might part forever—it hardly mattered. These moments, so vivid and intense, were as enduring and specific as a piece of music, and could be replayed over and over again.
>
> As they walked through a grove of poplar trees, the light speckled their arms. Above them cardinals, starlings, and chickadees called to one another. The lawn was dotted with dandelions and buttercups. This pleasant afternoon might be temporarily forgotten, but with the merest effort surely it could be called back in almost perfect detail.[31]

Yes, they're adulterers, but, look, Colwin seems to be insisting, look at the pleasures there are to be had in a life. And Colwin doesn't really punish her characters for their pleasures. Frank and Billy are never found out, their respective marriages continue on, Billy even has a baby—and that feels like "another marvelous thing"—so what is left for the lovers is to make sense of what their relationship meant and what their current relationships mean. In Chekhov's famous *The Lady with the Little Dog*, it is the final recognition of love that complicates everything, that makes what started as a light affair something painful and problematic. "How? How?" wonders Dmitry Dmitrich Gurov, in the closing moments of Chekhov's story, can things be made to work out, and he realizes "that the most complicated and difficult part was just beginning."[32] Granted, Billy has put her affair— the physical part of it—behind her when she comes to emotional peace, but it is an emotional peace that comes with a final recognition of love. Colwin leaves her character in just the opposite place that Chekhov leaves his. As Billy holds her infant son, we're told that Billy "felt her heart open and expand; she loved everyone—William, Grey, Penny, Francis. Her baby breathed against her."[33] When she looks up and thinks she sees her old lover, she starts, nonetheless, and then realizes it is only someone who resembles Frank, that she can love safely, should she choose. A thoughtful contentment is possible in this life, or so Colwin seems to be saying.

And is that mere sentimentality? Not to my mind. "Colwin carries it off," writes novelist Elizabeth Searle, "because she is so witty and her moment-by-moment observations are so sharp. (You've got to have some sort of Lennon/McCartney dark/light mix, don't you, or it's just too lightweight to pack any emotional punch.)"[34]

IN MY informal e-mail poll on happy writers, the only name that my friends consistently mentioned was Jane Austen. Lisa Zeidner, in starting a book review in the *New York Times,* once wrote, "If you want dour dysfunction in a novel, there's a huge menu. But if you hunger for happiness, the choices usually boil down to one: Jane Austen."[35] Now, in their own way, Austen's characters are plenty dysfunctional, though her heroines aren't, and her endings are happy. True, the pleasing happiness of Austen's ends come after novels that are arguably dark (though played lightly) in terms of human hypocrisy and greed. Still when the book is over, things have fallen into place: the girl gets her man, others get their just desserts. The heroine has learned the lesson she needed to learn about persuasion or romanticism or interfering in others' love lives.

Not that cheeriness is necessary for a happy end. "All works of art which deserve their name," writes Joseph Wood Crutch, "must have a happy end."[36] This doesn't disavow the "happiness," as Jean Thompson once noted, of an end that is "somber and satisfying." As she says, "We must be and *are* glad that Juliet dies and Lear is turned out into the storm."[37] The right end satisfies, and satisfaction makes us happy.

But in a literal sense, a felicitous or "right" ending is often *not* a happy ending. Cynthia Ozick's concentration camp story "The Shawl" is certainly a work of art, but I don't think anyone would argue that when Rosa's baby is pulled from her breast and thrown onto an electric fence we're dealing with a happy ending. It might be true—an accurate depiction of the kind of thing that happened during the Holocaust—but it is also mighty depressing. With Ozick's story, we're not, it's clear, in the realm of J. D. Salinger's "For Esmé—With Love and Squalor," where a man, damaged by war, exultantly tells a child pen pal that, essentially, he'll be all right in the end. Salinger's story feels more fanciful, less true than "The Shawl," and not only because of the happy ending. The story is lovely in its focus on the precocious charm of little Esmé, who presciently requires a correspondence from the damaged soldier X, but Esmé teeters on the edge (for the story's purpose and the soldier character's purpose) of the too good to be true.

In a cosmic sense, though, Salinger's story may be no happier than Ozick's. It's lighter, for sure, but not quite as satisfying. For the writer, pessimism and hope might not be as mutually exclusive as seems at first glance, or on first read.

In a 1986 interview, Margaret Atwood said, "When I finish a book I really like, no matter what the subject matter, or see a play or film, like Kurosawa's *Ran*, which is swimming in blood and totally pessimistic, but so well done, I feel very good. I do feel hope. . . . If you see something done very, very well, something that is true to itself, you can feel for two or three minutes that the clouds have parted and you've had a vision of something of what music or art or writing can do, at its best. A revelation of the full range of our human response to the world—that is, what it means to be human, on earth. That seems to be what 'hope' is about in relation to art. Nothing so simple as 'happy endings.'"[38]

STILL . . . sometimes the world is already too much with us, as in the days after September 11. Sometimes we do hunger for a literally, rather than a cosmically, happy book. My current favorite novel is W. G. Sebald's *Austerlitz,* a simply brilliant book about history, the construction of identity, memory, and more. It's not an easy read. It's largely a single paragraph, and its many ideas and interesting links between the patterns of consciousness, architecture, and history are complex. I'm glad that I read the book a few months ago instead of in the fall of 2001. In a large sense, in Atwood's sense, Sebald's is a hopeful book, but it is also exhausting and depressing. I read it on a train but would have liked to read it as I've read Walker Percy and other sad-sack favorites: in bed and propped up by a lot of pillows.

I listen to a lot of books on tape as I drive to and from work. Last fall, I listened to Diane Johnson's *Le Mariage*. Though the book has an arguably unhappy ending, it is a light read, a sort of silly book concerning expats and Parisians, all linked by love and the mystery of a stolen painting. Not a work that nears the level of Sebald's novel, but it was what I could handle at the time. "Sometimes," say the mothers of two of my son's friends, "I just want a feel-good movie." That's the sort of sentence that normally makes serious, literary me roll my eyes, but, of course, I can't say I don't know what they mean, can't say I haven't ever sought out—in literature or film—just the sort of pleasures that such a sentence implies.

IF CHEKHOV is right that we don't turn to fiction for answers, but to have questions posed, one way of considering the issue of happiness and consolation in art is to look at Barbara Moss's "The Rug Weaver," a story that deals with this very issue.

"The Rug Weaver" is about an Iranian Jew living with his son and daughter-in-law in Southern California. Ebrahim Nahavendi's present circumstances are rather idyllic. At least his immediate surrounds are comfortable and undemanding, all lush beauty and light. His family, particularly his daughter-in-law, Kimberly, is entirely welcoming. She means to make him happy in his new life. His old life was much darker. Though he more or less flourished as a somewhat otherworldly rug merchant working for his father-in-law in the shah's Iran, neither he nor his family fully survived the revolution. His father-in-law was taken from his rug shop and shot. Ebrahim was jailed for months, during which time he assumed he'd be released—like his father-in-law before him—to a bullet.

Given these twin tragedies, Ebrahim's always-nervous wife's hysteria gets the better of her. She continues to suffer even once the surviving members of her family are free and in Paris. There, she is placed, against her will (and with Ebrahim's consent), in a mental hospital, where she dies. Ebrahim, the somewhat dreamy son of a Talmudic scholar, had let himself be bought into a loveless (though respectful) marriage. He must live with the compromises he's made, the losses he's suffered, and the wounds he's inflicted.

And it isn't as if there is no tension in Ebrahim's present. He's got to figure out how to live in paradise. He's already figured out how to live in hell, or at least he had a method for saving himself while in prison. He became an artist, a weaver of rugs, only he wove not with fabric but with light, letting the bars of his jail cell serve as his loom. This doesn't exactly mean that he dreamed up a rug while in prison, for the emphasis—in the prison sections of Moss's story—is on the actual creation of a rug of light. At one point, Ebrahim reflects, like any artist wrestling with his or her material, on the difficulty of executing an idea. About the creation of a simple sun design, we are told that Ebrahim "had underestimated the difficulty of transferring it from his head to the lower left corner of the window; it required an effort of imagination that he felt too weak to make, a spasm that was almost physical, as if the object were lodged literally behind his eyes and he had to tear it loose."[39]

A rug of light—this is extraordinary enough—but Ebrahim's rug's design is also fantastic. It's a creation of Creation. (Ebrahim "should begin," he decides, "as God began, by separating light from dark.")[40] Ebrahim, a dabbler in Jewish mysticism, knows that he's going into forbidden territory, that his notions are entirely hubristic. A non-Jew might be interested in the Jewish proscription against plastic arts, which comes from the commandment against idolatry. Technically, for the observant Jew, any reproduction of the human image is suspect. This proscription applies to literature as well. Imitating the deity by depicting his creation—humans, in particular—is a great transgression. But, in his cellblock, Ebrahim persists nonetheless, embarking on an unabashed search for paradise.

The search starts with a phrase once spoken by Ebrahim's Talmudic scholar of a father: "Paradise is present in our time, but concealed."[41] My own limited understanding of Jewish mysticism—mostly gleaned from Adin Steinsaltz's beautiful book, *The Thirteen Petalled Rose*—suggests that this line refers to how the Godhead, the Supreme Being, creates through constriction, that is, that there is a world only because God chooses to limit himself. If He didn't, there would simply be divine plenitude and no creation. But Ebrahim's take on the sentence is a bit different. In his prison cell, he thinks, "If paradise is a state of mind, it can be found anywhere, even here. Shall I check the corners?"[42] And thus he has his first ecstatic encounter with artistic creation. He starts to make his rug, weaving a Persian knot in his head. Again, this is not a fictitious rug, for when Ebrahim opens his eyes, we're told, "the bars of the window were threaded with light."[43] While Ebrahim works, he pretends he doesn't know what he is doing, that he's not trying to make Eden, not trying "to replicate the grand design of God," but when he considers his work at the end of a day, he "exults shamelessly."[44]

Now, in the paradise of Southern California, Ebrahim's rug is . . . well, not gone exactly but not present either. If earlier Ebrahim wove his rug against the darkness of his prison circumstances, there is no similar frame in bright California, though Ebrahim darkens the apartment above his son's garage and imposes a physical darkness (in dress) and manner (he smokes) that is the opposite of his daughter-in-law's sunny, minimally shod, health-food-loving ways.

Kimberly herself seems like Eve, a true innocent, always hoisting platters of fresh fruit to her loved ones and living a physical, relatively unreflective life. Ebrahim is attracted to his daughter-in-law, though the attraction is subterranean. He imagines that "what he feels for his daughter-in-law is not sexual. Not *precisely* sexual."[45] In turn, Kimberly has desires of her own. Hers, too, are not precisely sexual, though she is clearly drawn to Ebrahim's sophistication—and seems to have some underground fantasies about Sami, Ebrahim's other son, still back in Paris. Perhaps he is a young version of Ebrahim?

What focuses the present-day tension in the story is Paris, or the idea of Paris. When Ebrahim was a boy, he dreamed of Paris, picturing it as a place where "horse-drawn carriages coexisted seamlessly with the latest racing cars." Paris was (in Ebrahim's imagination) what Southern California has turned out to be in fact: "one big garden."[46] And Paris had been Kimberly's dream as well, though a somewhat more prosaic one. She had wanted, before marriage, to be a flight attendant and live in Paris and have French boyfriends. Offhandedly—or perhaps not—Ebrahim (the snake!) suggests they go to Paris together.

In the end, though, Ebrahim rejects his own suggestion, understanding that he must choose between two Edens—the Eden in his head and an Eden in the world. Though the apple of Paris and Kimberly tempts him, he rejects it for his artistic creation. "The intellect of the man is forced to choose," writes William Butler Yeats, "Perfection of the life, or of the work."[47] Ebrahim chooses the work.

In prison, art literally provided Ebrahim with a way to live. Ebrahim's vocation worked "a purpose in him . . . greater than his fear."[48]

In California, art leads Ebrahim away from temptation to a kind of happiness. Beauty might not save the world, but in this story, art does save Ebrahim.

And this is good news, as Moss says of her own story: "Ebrahim transcends circumstances and makes art out of them. I'm not sure if my story is consoling, but for me it was a consolation to see that he had found a happiness and could make a clear choice in the end."[49]

IN MY private anthology of happy work, I'd put someone like Stuart Dybek, someone who writes about troubling or painful situations—the death of a brother, the loss of young love, the burning of a building—but is so celebratory, even ecstatic as he does so that he recalls me (as Colwin does) to the pleasures of life. And Dybek doesn't always work in a purely realistic mode to do this. Indeed, wildly imaginative work is—to my mind—often happy fiction, since one can't help but enjoy a virtuoso performance. I'd put a story like Victor Pelevin's "The Life and Adventures of Shed Number XII" in this category. It is, as the title suggests, about the life of a shed—an engagingly crazy premise in of itself, and one that busts open at story's close, when the shed essentially cheats death and breaks free of its worldly confines to become "something totally unreal," a riderless bike made of shed planks, flying through the air. "But strangest of all," Pelevin writes in his story's final page, "was that it glowed and flickered and changed color, sometimes turning transparent and then blazing with an unbearably intense brightness."[50] If Pelevin's story was a Disney—or Steven Spielberg—movie, this is where the schmaltzy music would start in, the triumph-of-the-shed music. But Pelevin is cleverer than that. He lets his creation disappear into the sky, he lets the one character who sees his creation—the director of Vegetable Shop 17—immediately forget it (as stunning as it was) and then reminds us that this director, sole repository of his vision, is "of no interest to us." And thus the story ends. When novelist/memoirist Christopher Noel thinks of happy work, he says that this is what he's most interested in, that is, "narrative playfulness, sheer exuberance of telling and describing, as in Nabokov."[51] Certainly a story like Pelevin's provides what novelist Tom Grimes wants out of "happy" fiction: "Happy requires some sense of the universe existing beyond our rational comprehension. If a story captures that, it's happy, and makes me happy too."[52]

AS A young girl, I thought I'd always be able to talk a suicide off of a balcony because I was sure I could name something a suicide would like to eat. Fritos? Wouldn't that make a person want to come in off a ledge? Salty, greasy Fritos, and as many as you wanted? In my twenties, the only time I ever really worried about myself was when I went through a period when I didn't even want to read. Now, was this a nervous breakdown or what? Because in the end, much of what I read makes me happy. Chekhov said that great art can never be depressing, and we know what he means, don't we? The truly depressing thing would be to never even record things, to not even try to capture human feeling, wherever it falls on the Happy-O-Meter.

And here's something that makes me even happier. It was a Colby undergraduate—one of the group who made me want to think about this issue in the first place—who came up with the quote with which I'd like to end my thoughts. It's from Seamus Heaney—again, the poets helping us poor fiction writers out. Of Yeats's poem "Man and the Echo," Heaney writes, it "manages to pronounce a final *Yes*. And the *Yes* is valuable because we can say of it what Karl Barth said of the enormous *Yes* at the centre of Mozart's music, that it has weight and significance because it overpowers and contains a *No*. Yeats's poetry, in other words, gives credence to the idea that courage is *some* good; it shows how the willful and unabashed activity of poetry itself is a manifestation of 'joy' and a redressal, in so far as it fortifies the spirit against assaults from the outside and temptations from within."[53]

A *yes* that can overpower and contain all the *nos* of the world? Is there such a thing? Does literature contain it? If so, that seems, to me, as good a reason as any to be happy all the time.

Notes

THE TRIGGER

1. John Fowles, "Notes on an Unfinished Novel," in *The Writers' Craft,* ed. John Hersey (New York: Knopf, 1981), 411.

2. Henry James, preface to *The Portrait of a Lady* (1909; Fairfield, N.J.: Kelley, 1976), vii.

3. Joan Didion, "Why I Write," *New York Times Magazine,* December 5, 1976.

4. Conversation with the author.

5. Joyce Carol Oates, "*Smooth Talk:* Short Story into Film," *Ontario Review* (1988), excerpted in *The Story and Its Writer: An Introduction to Short Fiction,* ed. Ann Charters (Boston: Bedford Books, 1995), 1478.

6. Qtd. in Ann Bernays and Pamela Painter, *What If?* (New York: HarperCollins, 1990), 31.

7. Henry James, preface to *The Spoils of Poynton* (1909; Fairfield, N.J.: Kelley, 1976), v.

8. Joan Didion, "Making Up Stories," in *The Writer's Craft: Hopwood Lectures, 1965–1981,* ed. Robert A. Martin (Ann Arbor: University of Michigan Press), 235.

9. George Eliot, "How I Came to Write Fiction," in *George Eliot's Life as Related in Her Letters and Journals,* ed. J. W. Cross (Boston: Estes and Lauriat, 1893–95).

10. Didion, "Why I Write."

11. Henry James, *The Art of Fiction,* excerpted in *The Writers' Craft,* ed. Hersey, 20.

12. Jane Smiley, qtd. in *American Voices: Best Short Fiction by Contemporary Authors,* ed. Sally Arteseros (New York: Pocket Books, 1992), 213.

13. James, preface to *Portrait of the Lady,* vii.

14. Philip Guston in *Philip Guston: A Life Lived* (New York: Blackwood, 1981).

15. John Cheever, "The Death of Justina," in *The Stories of John Cheever* (New York: Ballantine, 1982), 505–6.

16. Qtd. in Henri Troyat, *Chekhov,* trans. Michael Henry Heim (New York: Dutton, 1984, 1986), 76.

17. John Irving, "Getting Started," in *Writers on Writing,* ed. Robert Pack and Jay Parini (Hanover, N.H.: Middlebury College Press, University Press of New England, 1991), 98.

18. George Plimpton, ed., *Writers at Work: The Paris Review Interviews, Eighth Series* (New York: Penguin, 1988).

19. William Faulkner, "Interview at West Point," in *The Writer's Craft,* ed. Hersey, 38.

20. Didion, "Why I Write."

21. Conversation with the author.

22. Oscar Wilde, *The Importance of Being Earnest* (New York: Modern Library, 1980).

23. Rainer Maria Rilke, *Letters to a Young Poet,* trans. Stephen Mitchell (New York: Vintage, 1984, 1987), 7–8.

24. F. Scott Fitzgerald to Frances Turnbull (sophomore at Radcliffe), 1938, in *F. Scott Fitzgerald: A Life In Letters,* ed. Matthew J. Bruccoli (New York: Scribner's, 1994), 368.

25. Conversation with the author.

26. Joseph Conrad, "Author's Note," *Nostromo* (New York: Doubleday, 1927), xiv.

GETTING IN AND GETTING OUT

1. Alice Munro, "Miles City, Montana," in *The Progress of Love* (New York: Penguin, 1985, 1986), 84.

2. Andre Dubus, "Townies," in *Selected Stories* (Boston: David Godine, 1988), 359.

3. Cynthia Ozick, "Rosa," in *The Shawl* (New York: Vintage, 1980, 1983), 13.

4. Eberle Umbach, "Belly on a Stick," *Whole Earth Review* (fall 1987).

5. Conversation with the author.

6. Stuart Dybek, "Hot Ice," in *The Coast of Chicago* (New York: Knopf, 1990), 123.

7. Louise Erdrich,"Saint Marie," in *Love Medicine* (New York: Bantam, 1984, 1987), 40.

8. Robert Olen Butler, "A Good Scent from a Strange Mountain," in *A Good Scent from a Strange Mountain* (New York: Holt, 1992), 235.

9. Steve Stern, *Lazar Malkin Enters Heaven* (New York: Viking, 1986), 25.

10. Ernest Hemingway, "The Snows of Kilimanjaro," in *The Stories of Ernest Hemingway* (New York: Scribner's, 1938, 1966), 52.

11. Mona Simpson, "Lawns," in *The Vintage Book of American Short Stories,* ed. Tobias Wolff (New York: Vintage, 1993, 1994), 445.

12. Conversation with the author.

13. James Alan McPherson, "The Story of a Scar," in *Elbow Room* (Boston: Little, Brown, 1977), 97.

14. Margaret Atwood, "Uglypuss," in *Bluebeard's Egg and Other Stories* (Boston: Houghton Mifflin, 1986), 83.

15. Rust Hills, *Writing in General and the Short Story in Particular* (Boston: Mariner, 1977, 1987, 2000), 102.

16. David Quammen, "Walking Out," in *Matters of Life and Death,* ed. Tobias Wolff (Green Harbor, Mass.: Wampeter, 1983), 149.

17. Bernard Malamud, "The Last Mohican," in *The Stories of Bernard Malamud* (New York: Plume, 1984), 46.

18. Elizabeth Searle, "My Body to You," in *My Body to You* (Iowa City: University of Iowa Press, 1993), 1.

19. Anton Chekhov to A. N. Pleshcheyev, 1889 letter, qtd. in *Chekhov: Letters on the Short Story, the Drama, and Other Literary Topics,* ed. Louis S. Friedland (New York: Blom, 1964), 17.

20. Grace Paley, *The Collected Stories* (New York: Farrar, Straus, and Giroux, 1994), 232.

21. Vladimir Nabokov, "Chekhov's Prose," in *Critical Essays on Anton Chekhov,* ed. Thomas A. Eekman (Boston: Hall, 1989), 33.

22. Josip Novakovich, *Fiction Writer's Workshop* (Cincinnati: Story Press, 1995), 164.

23. Conversation with the author.

24. "Aaron Makes a Match," in Stern, *Lazar Malkin.*

25. Conversation with the author.

26. John Cheever, "The Country Husband," in *The Stories of John Cheever* (New York: Ballantine, 1982), 410.

27. Amy Hempel, "In the Garden Where Al Jolson Is Buried," in *Reasons to Live* (New York: Knopf, 1985), 37–53.

28. Butler, "Good Scent," 249.

29. V. S. Naipaul, *A House for Mr. Biswas* (New York: Penguin, 1961, 1969), 590.

30. Carol Shields, *The Stone Diaries* (New York: Viking, 1994), 361.

31. Harriet Doerr, *Stones for Ibarra* (New York: Penguin, 1984), 214.

32. Roddy Doyle, *Paddy Clarke Ha Ha Ha* (New York: Viking, 1993), 282.

33. Frank O'Connor, "The Guests of the Nation," in *Collected Stories* (New York: Knopf, 1981), 12.

34. Mary Gordon, introduction to James Joyce's "The Dead," in *You've Got to Read This,* ed. Ron Hansen and Jim Shepard (New York: HarperPerennial, 1994), 286.

SPEAKING OF STYLE

1. Stephen Minot, *Three Genres: The Writing of Fiction, Poetry, and Drama* (Englewood Cliffs, N.J.: Prentice-Hall, 1965).

2. Lorrie Moore, "People Like That Are the Only People Here," in *Birds of America* (New York: Knopf, 1998), 212.

3. Lorrie Moore, "How to Become a Writer," in *Self-Help* (New York: Knopf, 1985), 117.

4. Isaac Babel, "Guy de Maupassant," in *The Complete Works of Isaac Babel,* ed. Nathalie Babel, trans. Peter Constantine (New York: Norton, 2002), 681.

5. Konstantin Paustovsky, *The Story of a Life: Years of Hope,* trans. Manya Harari and Andrew Thompson (New York: Pantheon, 1968), 142–43.

6. Babel, "Guy de Maupassant," 681.

7. Gertrude Stein, "Poetry and Grammar," in *Lectures in America* (Boston: Beacon, 1935), 210–11.

8. Mary Stefaniak, "What We Talk about When We Talk about Style," *Iowa Journal of Library Studies* 7 (1986): 157.

9. Jonathan Swift, January 9, 1720, in *Letters to a Young Clergyman,* from John Bartlett, *Bartlett's Familiar Quotations,* 15th ed. (Boston: Little, Brown, 1855; 1980), 322.

10. Stefaniak, "What We Talk About," 157.

11. Raymond Carver, "Why Don't You Dance?" in *What We Talk about When We Talk about Love* (New York: Vintage, 1982), 5.

12. Qtd. in Pete Dexter, "The Old Man and the River," *Esquire,* June 1981, 89.

13. Stefaniak, "What We Talk About," 157.

14. William Strunk and E. B. White, *The Elements of Style,* 4th ed. (Boston: Allyn and Bacon, 1999), viii.

15. John Cheever, "Goodbye, My Brother," in *The Stories of John Cheever* (New York: Ballantine, 1982), 1.

16. Cheever, "Goodbye, My Brother," 23.

17. Stefaniak, "What We Talk About," 160–61.

18. William Faulkner, "Interview at West Point," in *The Writer's Craft,* ed. John Hersey (New York: Knopf, 1981), 41.

19. Henry James, *The Art of Fiction,* excerpted in *The Writers' Craft,* ed. Hersey (New York: Knopf, 1981), 20.

20. Aleksandar Hemon, "Passover," *Ploughshares* (fall 2002), 61.

21. Hemon, "Passover," 61.

22. George Saunders, "Jon," *New Yorker,* January 27, 2003.

23. George Orwell, "Politics and the English Language," in *Shooting an Elephant and Other Essays* (New York: Harcourt Brace, 1950), 85.

24. http://www.theatlantic.com/unbound/interviews/ba2000-05-17.html.

25. John Updike, "Varieties of Religious Experience," *The Atlantic,* November 2002. www.theatlantic.com/doc/prem/200211/updike

26. Babel, "Guy de Maupassant," 681.

27. Strunk and White, *Elements of Style,* 66–67.

28. www.theatlantic.com/unbound/interviews/ba2000-05-17.html.

29. Raymond Carver, "Train," in *Cathedral* (New York: Knopf, 1983), 154–55.

CRY, CRY, CRY

1. Leo Tolstoy, "What Is Art?" in *The Writer's Craft,* ed. John Hersey (New York: Knopf, 1981), 25–31.

2. Edna O'Brien, "It's a Bad Time Out There for Emotion," in *The Best Writing on Writing,* ed. Jack Heffron (Cincinnati: Story Press, 1994), 163.

3. O'Brien, "It's a Bad Time," 3.

4. Qtd. in Richard Hugo, *The Triggering Town* (New York: Norton, 1979), 7.

5. Emily Dickinson, "365", in *The Complete Poems of Emily Dickinson,* ed. Thomas H. Johnson (Boston: Little, Brown, 1960), 173.

6. Dickinson, "1640," in *Complete Poems,* 672.

7. Qtd. in Ted Solotaroff, "Writing in the Cold: The First Ten Years," in *A Few Good Voices in My Head* (New York: Harper and Row, 1981), 65.

8. James Baldwin, "Everybody's Protest Novel," in *Notes of a Native Son* (Boston: Beacon, 1949, 1955, 1983–84), 14.

9. All definitions from the *Oxford English Dictionary.*

10. Charles Dickens, *The Old Curiosity Shop* (London: Dent, 1907), 524.

11. Fred Kaplan, *Sacred Tears: Sentimentality in Victorian Literature* (Princeton: Princeton University Press, 1987), 16.

12. Kaplan, *Sacred Tears,* 38.

13. George G. Williams, *Readings for Creative Writers* (New York: Harper, 1938), 292.

14. Williams, *Readings,* 284.

15. David Huddle, *The Writing Habit* (Salt Lake City: Peregrine Smith Books, 1992), 126.

16. Stewart O'Nan, "Please Help Find," *Ploughshares* 25, nos. 2 and 3 (1999): 140.

17. O'Nan, "Please Help Find," 141.

18. O'Nan, "Please Help Find," 149.

19. Williams, *Readings,* 286.

20. Toni Cade Bambara, "Gorilla, My Love," in *Gorilla, My Love* (New York: Random House, 1972), 15.

21. Williams, *Readings,* 289.

22. Conversation with the author.

23. William Trevor, *Reading Turgenev,* in *Two Lives* (New York: Penguin, 1991), 220–21.

24. Trevor, *Reading Turgenev,* 2.

25. Conversation with the author.

26. T. S. Eliot, *The Sacred Wood* (London: Butler and Tanner, 1920), 100.

27. Tolstoy, "What Is Art?"

28. Dan Chaon, "The Illustrated Encyclopedia of the Animal Kingdom," in *Among the Missing* (New York: Ballantine, 2001), 120–21.

29. Oscar Hijuelos, *The Mambo Kings Play Songs of Love* (New York: Farrar, Straus and Giroux, 1989), 8.

30. Conversation with the author.

31. Janet Burroway, *Writing Fiction,* 5th ed. (New York: Longman, 2000), 281.

32. Conversation with the author.

33. Qtd. in Henri Troyat, *Chekhov* (New York: Dutton, 1986), 148.

34. Trevor, *Reading Turgenev,* 107.

35. Trevor, *Reading Turgenev,* 109.

36. Trevor, *Reading Turgenev,* 107.

37. Qtd. in Karsten Harries, *The Meaning of Modern Art* (Evanston, Ill.: Northwestern University Press, 1968), 78.

38. Harries, *Meaning,* 79.

39. Qtd. in Harries, *Meaning,* 79.

40. Milan Kundera, *The Art of the Novel* (New York: Harper and Row, 1988), 163.

CURIOUS ATTRACTIONS

1. Victoria Nelson, "The Strange History of the American Fantastic," *Agni Magazine* 36 (1992): 281–88.

2. David Young and Keith Hollaman, introduction to *Magical Realist Fiction* (New York: Longman, 1984), 1–2.

3. Qtd. in Jeanne Delbazre, "Magic Realism: The Energy of the Margins," in *Postmodern Fiction in Canada* (Amsterdam: Rodopi, 1992), 96.

4. Bernard Malamud, "The Jewbird," in *The Stories of Bernard Malamud* (New York: Farrar, Straus and Giroux, 1983), 144–54.

5. Delbazre, "Magic Realism," 75.

6. William Spindler, "Magic Realism: A Typology," *Forum for Modern Language Studies* 39, no. 1 (1993): 75.

7. Qtd. in Delbazre, "Magic Realism," 75.

8. Gabriel García Márquez, *One Hundred Years of Solitude,* trans. Gregory Rabassa (New York: HarperCollins, 1970), 1.

9. Spindler, "Magic Realism," 75.

10. Spindler, "Magic Realism," 76.

11. María-Elena Angulo, *Magic Realism: Social Context and Discourse* (New York and London: Garland Publishing, 1995), 4.

12. Alejo Carpentier, introduction to *El Reino de Este Mundo* (Caracas: Primer Festival del Libro Venezolano, 1974), 9.

13. Spindler, "Magic Realism," 76.

14. Alejo Carpentier, *The Kingdom of This World,* trans. Harriet de Onis (New York: Knopf, 1957), 28.

15. Gabriel García Márquez, "The Solitude of Latin America: Nobel Address, 1982," in *Gabriel García Márquez: New Readings,* ed. Bernard McGuirk and Richard Cardwell (New York: Cambridge University Press, 1987), 207–11.

16. Frederic Jameson, "On Magical Realism in Film," *Critical Inquiry* 12 (winter 1986): 311.

17. Carpentier, introduction.

18. Spindler, "Magic Realism," 82.

19. Bob Shacochis, "The Politics of Imagination," in *Point of Contact* (Syracuse University), reprinted in *Harper's,* November 1995.

20. Steve Stern, "Zelik Rithin and the Tree of Dreams," in *A Plague of Dreamers: Three Novellas* (New York: Scribner's, 1994).

21. Nelson, "Strange History," 284.

22. Nelson, "Strange History," 283–84.

23. Angel Flores, "Magic Realism in Spanish American Fiction," *Hispania,* 38, no. 2 (May 1955): 187–92.

24. Flores, "Magic Realism," 189.

25. Flores, "Magic Realism," 189.

26. Qtd. in Flores, "Magic Realism," 190.

27. Flores, "Magic Realism," 191.

28. Julio Cortázar, "Letter to a Young Lady in Paris," in *Blow-Up and Other Stories* (New York: Pantheon, 1985), 41.

29. Jorge Luis Borges, "The Aleph," in *The Aleph and Other Stories,* trans. Norman Thomas di Giovanni (New York: Dutton, 1970), 27–28.

30. Spindler, "Magic Realism," 82.

31. Victor Erlich, *Gogol* (New Haven: Yale University Press, 1969), 89.

32. Qtd. in Thais S. Lindstrom, *Nikolay Gogol* (New York: Twayne, 1974), 85.

33. Nicolai Gogol, "The Nose," in *The Overcoat and Other Tales of Good and Evil,* trans. David Magarshack (New York: Norton, 1965), 20.

34. Gabriel García Márquez, "A Very Old Man with Enormous Wings," in *Leaf Storm and Other Stories,* trans. Gregory Rabassa (New York: Harper and Row, 1972), 109.

35. García Márquez, "A Very Old Man," 110.

36. Gabriel García Márquez, *El Olor de la Guayaba: Conversaciones con Plinio Apuleyo Mendoza* (Barcelona: Editorial Bruguera, 1982), 90.

37. Richard Burgin, *Conversations with Jorge Luis Borges* (New York: Holt, Rinehart, and Winston, 1969), 130.

38. Martha Bayles, "Special Effects, Special Pleading," *New Criterion* 1 (1988): 38.

39. Julio Cortázar, "Axolotl," *Final del Juego* (Mexico City: Ed. Los Presentes, 1956), 161–69.

ASPECTS OF THE SHORT NOVEL

1. E. M. Forster, *Aspects of the Novel* (New York: Harcourt, Brace, and World, 1927, 1954), 43.

2. Conversation with the author.

3. Edith Wharton, *The Writing of Fiction* (London: Scribner's, 1925), 108.

4. Wharton, *Writing*, 102.

5. Conversation with the author.

6. Dean Flower, introduction to *Great Short Works of Henry James* (New York: Harper and Row, 1966), vii–viii.

7. Philip Gerard, *Writing a Book That Makes a Difference* (Cincinnati: Story Press, 2000), 171.

8. Howard Nemerov, "Composition and Fate in the Short Novel," in *Poetry and Fiction: Essays* (New Brunswick, N.J.: Rutgers University Press, 1963), 229.

9. Arnold B. Sklare, ed., *The Art of the Novella: Eight Short Novels* (New York: Macmillan, 1965), 1.

10. Ronald Paulson, ed., *The Modern Novelette* (Englewood Cliffs, N.J.: Prentice-Hall, 1965), viii.

11. Nemerov, "Composition and Fate," 235.

12. Paulson, *Modern Novelette*, ix.

13. Wallace Stegner, "Haunted by Waters: Norman Maclean," in *When the Bluebird Sings to the Lemonade Springs: Living and Writing in the West* (New York: Random House, 1992), 197.

14. William Kittredge and Annick Smith, "The Two Worlds of Norman Maclean: Interviews in Montana and Chicago," *TriQuarterly* 60 (spring–summer 1984): 416.

15. Qtd. in Pete Dexter, "The Old Man and the River," in *Norman Maclean*, ed. Ron McFarland and Hugh Nichols (Lewiston, Idaho: Confluence, 1988), 146.

16. *New York Times Book Review*, October 9, 1994, 7.

17. Conversation with the author.

18. W. B. Yeats, "The Choice," in *The Yeats Reader* (New York: Scribner's, 1997), 128.

19. Steven Millhauser, "The Little Kingdom of J. Franklin Payne," in *Little Kingdoms* (New York: Poseidon Press, 1993), 20.

20. Millhauser, "The Little Kingdom," 114.

21. Irving Howe, ed., *Classics of Modern Fiction: Eight Short Novels* (New York: Harcourt, Brace, and World, 1968), vii.

22. Conversation with the author.

23. Conversation with the author.

24. Lorrie Moore, *Who Will Run the Frog Hospital?* (New York: Knopf, 1994), 4.

25. Moore, *Who Will Run*, 5.

26. Qtd. in *Harpers Bazaar*, October 1994, 140.

27. Moore, *Who Will Run*, 18.

28. Caryn James, "I Feel His Lach of Love for Me," *New York Times Book Review* (Oct. 9, 1994).

29. Wharton, *Writing*, 103.

30. Nemerov, "Composition and Fate," 245.

31. Conversation with the author.

32. For more on the history of the novella, see Charles May, "The Novella," in *Critical Survey of Long Fiction: English Language Series*, ed. Frank N. Magill (Englewood Cliffs, N.J.: Salem, 1983), 3213–39.

33. Nemerov, "Composition and Fate," 239.

34. Moore, *Who Will Run*, 25.

35. Qtd. in William Maxwell, *So Long, See You Tomorrow* (Boston: Godine, 1980), 25–27.

36. Maxwell, *So Long,* 25.

37. Maxwell, *So Long,* 26.

BORDER GUARD

1. John Hersey, *Hiroshima* (New York: Knopf, 1946), 21.

2. John Cheever, "Goodbye, My Brother," in *You've Got to Read This,* ed. Ron Hansen and Jim Shepard (New York: HarperPerennial, 1994), 153.

3. Stuart Dybek, "Fiction," *Tin House* 1, no. 1 (spring 1999).

4. Don Lee, "About Stuart Dybek," *Ploughshares* 24, no. 1 (spring 1998): 197.

5. Stuart Dybek, "Blight," in *The Coast of Chicago* (New York: Knopf, 1990), 42.

6. Dybek, "Hot Ice," in *Coast of Chicago,* 124.

7. Mike Nickel and Adrian Smith, "An Interview with Stuart Dybek," *Chicago Review* 43, no. 1 (winter 1997): 102.

8. Dybek, "Hot Ice," 131.

9. Beryl Markham, *West with the Night* (San Francisco: North Point Press, 1983), 106.

10. Dybek, "Hot Ice," 106.

11. Dybek, "Hot Ice," 124.

12. Dybek, "Hot Ice," 124.

13. Stuart Dybek, interview by Fred Shafer (Northwestern University), June 24, 2000.

14. Dybek, "Hot Ice," 124.

15. Dybek, "Hot Ice," 124–25.

16. Dybek, "Hot Ice," 129.

17. Dybek, "Hot Ice," 131.

18. Dybek interview with Shater.

19. Susan Stamberg, ed., *The Wedding Cake in the Middle of the Road: Twenty-three Variations on a Theme* (New York: Norton, 1992), 25–26.

20. Nickel and Smith, "Interview."

21. Dybek, "Hot Ice," 133.

22. Dybek, "Hot Ice," 129.

23. Dybek, "Hot Ice," 126.

24. Dybek, "Hot Ice," 130.

25. Dybek, "Hot Ice," 138–39.

26. Dybek, "Hot Ice," 136.

27. Dybek, "Hot Ice," 142.

28. Dybek, "Hot Ice," 143–44.

29. Dybek, "Hot Ice," 144.

30. Dybek, "Hot Ice," 126.

31. Dybek, "Hot Ice," 126–27.

32. Dybek, "Hot Ice," 127.

33. Dybek, "Hot Ice," 128.

34. Nickel and Smith, "Interview."

35. Dybek, "Hot Ice," 145.

36. Robert Wilder, "Surprise, Inevitability, and Unity: Plotting the Path to Resolution in Cheever and Dybek" (master's degree essay, Warren Wilson College, 1998), 17.

37. Dybek, "Hot Ice," 154.

38. Dybek, "Hot Ice," 154–55.

39. Dybek interview.

40. Dybek, "Hot Ice," 155.

41. Dybek, "Hot Ice," 123.

42. Dybek, "Hot Ice," 157.

43. Dybek, "Hot Ice," 156.

44. Dybek, "Hot Ice," 124.

45. Dybek, "Hot Ice," 158.

46. James Galvin, "Cartography," in *Elements* (Port Townsend: Copper Canyon Press, 1988), 18.

STAND BACK

1. E. M. Forster, *Aspects of the Novel* (New York: Harcourt Brace Jovanovich, 1927, 1955), 47.

2. Percy Lubbock, *The Craft of Fiction* (New York: Cape and Smith, 1929, 1931), 251.

3. Lubbock, *Craft,* 254.

4. Lubbock, *Craft,* 252.

5. Lubbock, *Craft,* 254.

6. Lubbock, *Craft,* 255.

7. Lubbock, *Craft,* 256.

8. Lubbock, *Craft,* 258.

9. Deborah Eisenberg, "The Girl Who Left Her Sock on the Floor," in *All Around Atlantis: Stories* (New York: Farrar, Straus and Giroux, 1997), 8.

10. Margaret Atwood, "Wilderness Tips," in *Wilderness Tips* (New York: Doubleday, 1991), 183–84.

11. Angela Carter, "The Courtship of Mr. Lyon," in *Burning Your Boats: The Collected Short Stories* (New York: Holt, 1996), 144.

12. Elizabeth Strout, *Amy and Isabelle* (New York: Random House, 1998), 3.

13. Strout, *Amy and Isabelle,* 138.

14. Conversation with the author.

15. John Gardner, *The Art of Fiction: Notes on Craft for Young Writers* (New York: Knopf, 1983, 1984), 111.

16. Richard Cohen, *Writer's Mind: Crafting Fiction* (Lincolnwood, Ill.: NTC, 1995), 103.

17. Jerome Stern, *Making Shapely Fiction* (New York: Norton, 1991).

18. Akhil Sharma, "Surrounded by Sleep," in *The Best American Short Stories,* ed. Sue Miller (Boston: Houghton Mifflin, 2002), 304.

19. David Schnarch, *Passionate Marriage* (New York: Henry Holt, 1997), 65.

20. Conversation with the author.

21. E. B. White, *Essays of E. B. White* (New York: Harper Colophon, 1979), 261.

22. Conversation with the author.

23. Mario Vargas Llosa, *Letters to a Young Novelist,* trans. Natasha Wimmer (New York: Farrar, Straus and Giroux, 1997, 2002), 50.

24. Vargas Llosa, *Letters,* 75.

25. Vargas Llosa, *Letters,* 75.

26. Rick Russo, "In Defense of Omniscience," in *Bringing the Devil to His Knees: The Craft of Fiction and the Writing Life*, ed. Charles Baxter and Pete Turchi (Ann Arbor: University of Michigan Press, 2001), 17.

CHEER UP—WHY DON'T YOU?

1. National Public Radio, *Morning Edition*, October 19, 2001.
2. National Public Radio, *Morning Edition*, October 29, 2001.
3. Susan Stamberg, "Music for America: Artists Pick Tunes to Inspire and Heal," www.npr.org/news/specials/response/home_front/features/2001/oct/011019.stamberg.music.html.
4. National Public Radio, September 20, 2001.
5. Alexander Solzhenitsyn, 1970 Nobel Lecture, reprinted in *The Writer's Craft*, ed. John Hersey (New York: Knopf, 1974, 1981), 143.
6. Qtd. on National Public Radio, *Morning Edition*, November 8, 2001.
7. Bill Roorbach, "A Dead Character," *Colby Magazine* (spring 2002): 64.
8. *Publishers Weekly*, 2001; available at www.amazon.com.
9. Emily Dickinson, "42," in *The Complete Poems of Emily Dickinson* (Boston: Little, Brown, 1960), 24.
10. John Donne, "XVII Meditation," in *Devotions upon Emergent Occasions*, in *John Donne*, ed. John Carey (New York: Oxford University Press, 1990), 344.
11. William Stafford, "The Way It Is," in *The Way It Is: New and Selected Poems* (St. Paul, Minn.: Graywolf, 1998).
12. Mary Oliver, "In Blackwater Woods," in *Contemporary American Poetry*, 4th ed., ed. A. Poulin Jr. (Boston: Houghton Mifflin, 1985), 393.
13. Janet Burroway, *Writing Fiction: A Guide to Narrative Craft*, 5th ed. (New York: Longman, 2000), 29.
14. Nick Gaubinger, Colby alumnus.
15. Henry Munter, Colby alumnus.
16. Charles Baxter, *Burning down the House: Essays on Fiction* (St. Paul, Minn.: Graywolf, 1997), 170.
17. Burroway, *Writing Fiction*, 29.
18. Burroway, *Writing Fiction*, 33. Burroway credits her notions on this subject to dramatist Claudia Johnson.
19. Conversation with the author.
20. Bill Roorbach, "Big Bend," in *Big Bend: Stories* (Athens: University of Georgia Press, 2001), 172.
21. Jon Wilson, "On Finding Our Voice and Leaving Our Mark," www.hopemag.com/Pages/Jon.editorials-pages/16.html.
22. Jean Thompson, "Happy Endings," Warren Wilson Lecture, July 1989, Warren Wilson College—MFA Program for Writers, North Carolina.
23. Flannery O'Connor, "The Nature and Aim of Fiction," in *The Writer's Craft*, ed. Hersey, 47.
24. Conversation with the author.
25. Margaret Atwood, "Happy Endings," in *The Contemporary American Short Story*, ed. B. Minh Nguyen and Porter Shreve (New York: Pearson Longman, 2004), 18.
26. John Cheever, "A Worm in the Apple," in *The Stories of John Cheever* (New York: Ballantine, 1982), 338–39.

27. Cheever, "Worm," 342.

28. Laurie Colwin, *Happy All the Time* (New York: Knopf, 1978).

29. Laurie Colwin, *Another Marvelous Thing* (New York: Knopf, 1986), 62.

30. Colwin, *Another Marvelous Thing*, 31.

31. Colwin, *Another Marvelous Thing*, 53–54.

32. Anton Chekhov, "The Lady with the Little Dog," in *Anton Chekhov: Stories*, translated by Richard Pevear and Larissa Volokhonsky (New York: Bantam, 2000), 376.

33. Colwin, *Another Marvelous Thing*, 130.

34. E-mail correspondence from Elizabeth Searle.

35. Lisa Zeidner, "Josie and the Psychopaths," review of Jean Thompson's *Wild Blue Yonder*, *New York Times Book Review*, December 30, 2001.

36. Qtd. in Thompson, "Happy Endings."

37. Thompson, "Happy Endings."

38. Interview with Margaret Atwood in Geoff Hancock, *Canadian Writers at Work: Interviews with Geoff Hancock* (London: Oxford University Press, 1988).

39. Barbara Moss, "Rug Weaver," in *The Best American Short Stories, 2001*, ed. Barbara Kingsolver and Katrina Kenison (Boston: Houghton Mifflin, 2001), 160–61.

40. Moss, "Rug Weaver," 160.

41. Moss, "Rug Weaver," 157.

42. Moss, "Rug Weaver," 157.

43. Moss, "Rug Weaver," 158.

44. Moss, "Rug Weaver," 161–62.

45. Moss, "Rug Weaver," 173.

46. Moss, "Rug Weaver," 164

47. W. B. Yeats, "The Choice," in *Selected Poems and Three Plays*, 3d ed. (New York: Collier, 1931, 1932, 1986), 128.

48. Moss, "Rug Weaver," 169.

49. Conversation with the author.

50. Victor Pelevin, "The Life and Adventures of Shed Number XII," in *The Art of the Story*, ed. Daniel Halpern (New York: Viking, 1999), 501.

51. E-mail correspondence from Christopher Noel.

52. E-mail correspondence from Tom Grimes.

53. Seamus Heaney, "Joy of Night: Last Things in the Poetry of W. B. Yeats and Phillip Larkin," in *The Redress of Poetry* (New York: Noonday, 1996), 163.

Text design by Jillian Downey
Typesetting by Huron Valley Graphics, Ann Arbor, Michigan
Text font: Monotype Bulmer
Display font: Interstate

The font Bulmer was originally designed in 1792 by William
Martin, and Monotype Bulmer was created for American Type
Founders in 1928 by Morris Fuller Benton.

—Courtesy www.adobe.com

Interstate was designed by Tobias Frere-Jones in 1993–94 for Font
Bureau.

—Courtesy www.identifont.com and www.fontbureau.com